*Law*Basics

COMMERCIAL LAW

SECOND EDITION

AUSTRALIA
Law Book Co.
Sydney

CANADA and USA
Carswell
Toronto

HONG KONG
Sweet & Maxwell Asia

NEW ZEALAND
Brookers
Wellington

SINGAPORE and MALAYSIA
Sweet & Maxwell Asia
Singapore and Kuala Lumpur

*Law*Basics

COMMERCIAL LAW

SECOND EDITION

By

Nicholas J.M. Grier, M.A., LL.B., W.S., F.R.S.A.,

Solicitor,
Lecturer in Law,
Napier University

THOMSON
™
W. GREEN

Published in 2003 by

W. Green & Son Ltd
21 Alva Street
Edinburgh EH2 4PS

www.wgreen.co.uk

Reprinted 2005

Printed in Great Britain by Athenaeum Press Ltd,
Gateshead, Tyne & Wear

No natural forests were destroyed to make this product;
Only farmed timber was used and replanted

A CIP catalogue record for this book is available from the British Library

ISBN 0 414 01537 1

CONTENTS

TABLE OF CASES

1. SALE AND SUPPLY OF GOODS

THE NEED FOR LEGISLATION

Traditionally, the sale of goods was regulated by the old Roman law maxim of *caveat emptor*—let the buyer beware. As this was not always very satisfactory for the consumer, legislation was introduced to modernise the law, resulting in the Sale of Goods Act 1979. Other legislation that provides further rights for the consumer includes the Unfair Contract Terms Act 1977, the Sale and Supply of Goods Act 1994, the Consumer Credit Act 1974, the Consumer Protection Act 1987 and the Unfair Terms in Consumer Contracts Regulations 1999, introduced following the 1993 EC Council Directive on Unfair Terms in Consumer Contracts. In addition, the Sale and Supply of Goods to Consumer Regulations 2002 implement the 1999 EU Directive on the Sale of Consumer Goods and Associated Guarantees.

THE SALE OF GOODS ACT 1979 ("SOGA")

In order to understand SOGA it is worth understanding the various definitions used throughout SOGA, and indeed throughout the rest of this Chapter.

Definitions

Goods means corporeal moveables, which in Scotland means physical, tangible and transportable assets including things growing on or subsisting within land and which can be detached or extracted from land in order to be sold (SOGA, ss.61). The term "goods" does not include money, except in the context of antique coins and banknotes. It is not entirely clear whether or not computer programs contained on disks fall within the definition of "goods" (as stated in *St Albans City and District Council v International Computers Ltd* (1995)), or are a species of material which is neither goods nor any other legally recognised form of asset (*Beta Computers (Europe) Ltd v Adobe Systems (Europe) Ltd* (1996)).

A significant feature of goods is whether they are existing, ascertained and specific goods selected by the buyer, or *unascertained* goods, which are goods not specially chosen or identified by or for the buyer but which are or have been available to the buyer for purchase. When a buyer personally selects a kilo of carrots which he presents to the greengrocer for purchase, he has entered into a contract for specific or ascertained goods: if he sends some money to the greengrocer and asks the greengrocer to send him 7 kilos of best porridge oats, the contract is for the sale of unascertained goods up to the moment when the greengrocer

1

selects the porridge oats and sets them aside for the buyer, whereupon the goods become ascertained goods. *Appropriation* is the term used to describe the process of selecting, setting aside or otherwise identifying the goods for the buyer with the buyer's assent.

Goods do not need to exist at the time of sale: if the goods have yet to be obtained or manufactured, they are called *future goods* (SOGA, s.5).

A *sale* is defined in SOGA, s.2 as a contract by which the seller transfers or agrees to transfer the property in goods to the buyer for a money consideration, called the price. Accordingly a transfer which is reciprocated by a swap is not a sale but a form of barter and is outwith SOGA, since SOGA only deals with payment using money. Sale includes the concept of an immediate transfer or a future transfer ("agreement to transfer").

Property means the right of ownership. Ownership is different from possession. A person may own a wheelbarrow, but if he lends that wheelbarrow to a friend the friend has possession but not ownership.

A contract of sale of goods may be *absolute* or *conditional* (SOGA, s.2(3)). An absolute contract of sale is one where the property is transferred without anything needing to be done first. A conditional sale is one where some act needs to be fulfilled, or some time needs to have elapsed before the sale can take place. Where the transfer of the property is to take place after the completion of some act, or after a period of time, the contract is not a contract of sale, but an *agreement to sell* (SOGA, s.2(5)). An agreement to sell turns into a sale once the conditional act has been performed or the requisite time has elapsed (SOGA, s.2(6)). For example, the conditional act might be putting the goods into a deliverable state. Once the goods are in a deliverable state, the property in the goods transfers to the buyer.

When goods are said to be in a *deliverable state* the seller has placed the goods in such a state that the buyer is bound under the terms of his contract to take delivery of them (SOGA, s.18, Rule 3). Equally if goods are not in a deliverable state, the purchaser is not bound to accept the goods (unless the contract says otherwise).

Breach of contract occurs where a term of the contract is broken by one of the parties to the contract. If a term of the contract is broken by the seller, the buyer is entitled to claim damages for his loss (SOGA, s.15B(1)(a)), but if it is a very serious breach of a term (known as a material breach) the buyer is entitled to reject the goods (*i.e.* to send them back to the seller without payment) and to treat the contract as repudiated (*i.e.* to refuse to recognise the continued existence of the contract) (SOGA, s.15B(1)(b)).

A *material* breach is, as stated above, a significant or serious breach as opposed to a trivial or minor breach of a term of the contract. It is clearly difficult to give a categorical definition of what is material and what is not. In order to give guidance on this issue, SOGA, s.15B(2) states that in a consumer contract (to be explained later) any breach by the seller of a term in the contract as to the quality of the goods or their fitness for the purpose for which they were supplied (SOGA, s.15B(2)(a)) is a material breach. Within SOGA, s.15B(2) there are further occasions which are deemed to be material breaches. If a seller sells his goods by description, by perhaps advertising that he has a large quantity of a particular commodity which he describes as being of best quality and newly made, or if he displays a sample of his wares, there is an assumption that the actual goods will indeed entirely correspond with the seller's description and that the bulk of the goods will correspond with the sample. If it turns out that the goods are not of best quality nor new stock, or that the sample is unrepresentative of the inferior bulk, the consumer buyer may treat the goods' deficiencies as a material breach of a term of the contract, and is therefore entitled to reject the goods and claim his money back. SOGA s.15B applies only within Scotland.

A *consumer contract* is defined in the Unfair Contract Terms Act 1977 ("UCTA") as one where: (a) either the seller or the buyer is a consumer (*i.e.* someone not dealing, or holding himself out as dealing, in the course of a business) and the other party is dealing in the course of a business; and (b) the goods which form the subject of the contract are goods that are of a type ordinarily supplied for private use or consumption (UCTA, s.25(1)). The emphasis in this definition lies in the consumer not having a business dealing in the goods. The definition of "consumer" can in some circumstances even include a non-trading limited company or a charitable association. If there is a dispute about the nature of the consumer contract, it is for the party who says that the contract is not a consumer contract to prove that this is the case (UCTA, s.25(1)).

Risk is the term used to denote the exposure of the goods to the danger of loss or damage. From the moment a buyer accepts the risk in goods transferred or to be transferred to him, he should insure against the loss or destruction of the goods; and likewise where the risk lies with the seller he will be responsible for maintaining the goods up to the moment of transfer of risk.

Damages is the term used to describe the amount the court may award to cover the difference in value between the value of the contract if it had taken place properly and what the actual value turned out to be. In the context of a seller's breach of contract, it is the estimated loss to the buyer directly and naturally resulting, in the ordinary course of events, from the breach (SOGA, s.53A(1)). Damages in general aim to restore or bring the claimant to the position he ought to be in if the contract is performed properly, but damages are not meant to be penal in nature. Damages will normally amount to the cost of repair or upgrading to the expected standard, or the value of the loss occasioned by the delay or other fault. Interest is usually allowable as part of the damages. Where there has been bodily injury or consequential damage to property as a result of the faulty goods, there may be damages for these as well (SOGA, s.53A), though such damages are: (a) only available to the buyer and not to others who may be affected by the faulty goods; and (b) may only be claimed against the seller. The seller may not always be in a position to meet a sizeable claim and may in any case may not have manufactured the faulty goods. In that case it may be possible to make a claim for damages against persons other than the seller, such as the manufacturer. Such a claim could not be made under SOGA, but under the Consumer Protection Act 1987, discussed later in this Chapter. Unless the buyer has specifically drawn the seller's attention to matters which are important to the buyer (such as the need for the supplied goods to be ready by a certain date because some other matter was dependent on the goods being ready), the seller will not normally be liable for any further economic loss arising out of the seller's delay or fault (*Hadley v Baxendale* (1854)).

EXPRESS AND IMPLIED TERMS

In contracts of sale there are usually *express* terms, which are ones clearly spelt out, and *implied* terms, which are not. An implied term is one that is deemed to be in the contract unless it is specifically disapplied in the actual contract, and even then the attempt to contract out of the implied term may in certain circumstances be declared void by the courts. The implied terms in SOGA, ss.12, 13, 14 and 15 all impose strict liability, which means that irrespective of any reasonable precautions the seller may have taken, if the seller breaches the implied terms he will be liable, and it does not matter whose fault caused the breach. If the contract is silent on any of the undernoted matters the implied terms will automatically apply. The implied terms are that:

(a) The seller has the right to sell the goods (SOGA, s.12(1)). So if the goods turn out to be stolen, the buyer may sue the seller for breach of this right, notwithstanding any intervening circumstances. This took place in *Rowland v Divall* (1923), where the buyer of a car was successfully able to have his entire purchase price returned to him from the seller when it was discovered that the car was stolen and had to be returned to its true owner, notwithstanding that in the meantime the buyer had had three months of driving in the car.

(b) Up to the moment when the property is to pass to the buyer, there is no charge or encumbrance over the goods, or if there is, it must be disclosed to the buyer (SOGA, s.12(2)(a)). A "charge or encumbrance" is a term of English law and means a right over the goods in favour of somebody else. If a seller sold his car which was in a garage being repaired, the buyer might find when he went to pick it up that the garage owner would not release the car until the seller's repair bill was paid, a matter the seller had forgotten to tell the buyer; in this event the buyer could sue the seller for breach of this term because of the undisclosed lien over the car in favour of the garage owner.

(c) Irrespective of the time that the property is to pass, the buyer may have quiet possession of the goods except to the extent of any disclosed charge or encumbrance (SOGA, s.12(2)(b)). In *Niblett Ltd v Confectioners Materials Co.* (1921), the buyers found that the labelling on tins purchased from the seller infringed a recognised trademark. The labels had thus to be removed and the buyers successfully sued the sellers for breach of the requirement of "quiet possession".

(d) Where either from the terms of the contract, or from the circumstances surrounding the contract, it is apparent that the seller or a disclosed further person does not have full title (*i.e.* ownership or the right to sell), provisions (a), (b) and (c) continue to apply but the seller or other disclosed further person will only be liable to the extent of what he has not disclosed (SOGA, s.12(3),(4), and (5)).

Unless it is made clear by the seller to the buyer that the seller is only transferring such (limited) right as he may have (as, say, when a receiver is selling a company's assets under the powers given to him under a floating charge (SOGA, s.12(3))), any attempt to contract out of SOGA, s.12 is automatically void under UCTA, s.20(1)(a) (as further discussed under "Exclusion of implied terms" below).

Further implied terms are that:

(e) Unless the contract of sale specifically says so, a stipulation as to when payment for the goods must be made is not deemed to be "of the essence of the contract" (*i.e.* a material matter which will entitle the seller to claim that the contract has been breached (SOGA, s.10(1))).

(f) Goods sold by description will correspond with their description (SOGA, s.13(1)). The bulk of goods should correspond with any sample (as well as with their description if appropriate) (SOGA, s.13(2)) and even if a buyer selects his goods, his purchase may if necessary still be a sale by description if the buyer has relied on a description.

(g) Where goods are sold in the course of a business (but not necessarily otherwise), the goods supplied must be of "satisfactory quality" (SOGA, s.14(2)). "Satisfactory" is defined as meeting the standard that a reasonable person would regard as satisfactory, taking account of the description of the goods, the price (where relevant) and all other relevant circumstances (SOGA, s.14(2A)). "Quality" means the state and condition of the goods (SOGA, s.14(2B)), taking into account the fitness for the purpose for which the goods were supplied, the goods' appearance and finish, freedom from minor defects, safety and durability (SOGA, s.14(2B)(a) to (e)). However, if defects or unsatisfactory matters are especially drawn to the buyer's attention, or where the buyer examines the goods and he ought to have noticed the defects, or in the case of a sample if a reasonable examination of the sample would have made the defects apparent, the protection afforded by SOGA, s.14(2) as to satisfactory quality is withdrawn (SOGA, s.14(2C)). Under SOGA s.14(2D) the "relevant circumstances" referred to in s.14(2A) include any advertising and labelling, thereby requiring that goods conform to what their producers or retailers say about those goods.

(h) Where the buyer explains to the seller (which word in this context also includes credit broker) the purpose for which the goods are being bought, the goods must be reasonably fit for that purpose (even if that purpose is not the usual use for those goods) *unless* circumstances show that the buyer was not relying on the seller's skill and judgment in satisfying that purpose or where it was unreasonable of him to rely on the seller's skill and judgment (SOGA, s.14(3)) (*Griffiths v Peter Conway Ltd* (1939)). A further feature of s.14(3) is that it applies to any seller of any goods in the course of a business, even if the goods in question are not those normally sold by the seller (*London Borough of Southwark v Charlesworth* (1983)).

(i) The above terms apply to a seller's agents in the course of the seller's business, and to agents for sellers not in the course of business, unless the fact that the seller is not in the course of business is already known to the buyer, or the fact of the seller's not being in business is brought to the attention of the buyer (SOGA, s.14(5)).

(j) Where there is a sale by sample, the bulk will correspond with the sample in quality and the goods will be free from any defect making the quality of the goods unsatisfactory, which would not be apparent on a reasonable examination of the sample (SOGA, s.15).

The exclusion of implied terms

It is not possible in any contract of sale to which SOGA applies to contract out of SOGA, s.12 (UCTA, s.20(1)) except, as stated above, to the extent that someone who does not have full title discloses his title as being less than full and discloses all charges in which case the only person who may destroy the buyer's possession of the goods is a disclosed holder of a charge (SOGA, s.12(4), (5)). It is also not possible to contract out of the provisions of SOGA, ss.13 to 15 (referred to in paragraphs (f) to (j) above) in a consumer contract (UCTA, s.20 (2)), though it is possible to do so in a commercial or non-consumer contract if the relevant contracting-out clause is fair and reasonable as defined in UCTA, s.24. This states that to define what is fair and reasonable, regard should be had to the circumstances known to, or which ought reasonably to have been known to, the parties at the time the contract was made. Reference may also be made to UCTA, Schedule 2 which lays down various guidelines as to: (a) the abuse of any strength of bargaining power; (b) the effect of any inducements to accept the contracting out clause; (c) normal business practice in the trade concerned or between the parties; (d) the practicality of compliance with any condition without which liability would be excluded; and (e) whether the goods were specially made or adapted to the buyer's particular order.

As regards the contracting out from implied terms (other than those specified in the previous paragraph), it is open to the parties to make such provisions as they choose, either expressly, by course of dealing, or by "such usage as binds both parties to the contract", being actions which indicate that both parties do intend to be bound by any contracting-out of the relevant implied terms and have an interest in being contracted out (SOGA, s.55(1)).

Further exclusion clauses
Under the Unfair Terms in Consumer Contracts Regulations 1999 ("UTCCR"), where consumers are required to enter into contracts where the opportunity for individual negotiation is not available (as in standard term contracts for such things as satellite televisions, portable telephones, etc.), consumers will not be bound where a non-negotiable term is "unfair" (UTCCR reg.8). Unfairness is judged by the criteria of being contrary to the requirements of good faith, being significantly in favour of the non-consumer party to the contract, and being detrimental to the consumer (UTCCR, reg.5(1)), although the courts are also required to take account of the nature of the goods and services referred to in the contract and to all the circumstances attending the conclusion of the contract (UTCCR, reg.6(1)). The seller or supplier must ensure that each written term of the contract is expressed in plain language intelligible to the consumer (UTCCR, reg.7(1)). If a term is ambiguous or unclear, the term will be construed in favour of the consumer (UTCCR, reg.7(2)).

CAPACITY TO BUY AND SELL

Not everyone is legally empowered to enter into contracts. Some individuals are *incapax* which means that by virtue of mental incapacity or other cause they are incompetent to contract. Where such individuals are sold necessaries (*i.e.* items such as food, drink and clothing) they must pay (and indeed are only obliged to pay) a reasonable price for them (SOGA, s.3(2)). The law on sales to children is regulated by the Age of Legal Capacity (Scotland) Act 1991 ("ALC"). Children below the age of 16 have no contractual capacity and their guardians (normally their parents) must act on their behalf. However, below the age of 16 it is acceptable for them to enter into contracts appropriate to their age and on terms that are "not unreasonable" (ALC, s.2(1)). Children aged 16 or over may enter into contracts of sale and purchase in the normal manner, except that between the ages of 16 and 18 if a contract is prejudicial to the child's interest the courts may set it aside at any stage up to the child's 21st birthday if a prudent adult would not have entered into the contract on the terms that the child suffered (ALC, s.3(1),(2)). If the child has lied about his age in order to enter the contract he will not be protected, and if he is in the course of a business he also loses the protection of the statute (ALC, s.3(3)).

FORMATION OF CONTRACTS OF SALE

Contracts for sale may be made verbally, in writing, by a combination of these means or may be inferred from the actions of the parties to the sale (SOGA, s.4). In any event the implied terms, referred to above, are deemed to be part of the contract of sale (except where variation of the implied terms is both agreed by the parties and permissible, which in the case of consumer contracts it may not be). As with all contracts, there must be *consensus in idem* (agreement on the same matters), a buyer and a seller, both with the necessary legal capacity, a price (which in the absence of any other agreement must be reasonable under the circumstances (SOGA, s.8)) and goods (present or future) to be transferred along with the property in the goods. Where specific goods have perished without the knowledge of the seller before or at the time that the contract is made, there are clearly no goods so the contract is void (SOGA, s.6) and no contract of any sort exists. Where there is an agreement to sell specific goods and goods subsequently perish through no fault of the buyer or seller before the risk passes to the buyer, the agreement is "frustrated" (*i.e.* cannot be brought to fruition) or avoided, the contract terminated, the seller has no obligation to deliver the goods (SOGA, s.7) and any money the buyer had given to the seller for the now perished goods would have to be returned to the buyer. This rule does not apply in the case of unascertained goods, since the seller ought to be able to produce more (unperished) goods from his warehouse. As stated above goods generally must be of satisfactory quality and fit for the relevant purpose for which they were acquired.

When does the buyer get the property in the goods?
This depends whether or not the goods are unascertained. If the goods are unascertained, no property in the goods passes to the buyer until the goods are ascertained (SOGA, s.16). Where the goods are specific or ascertained, the property in the goods passes when the parties intend the property to pass. This will normally be established by the terms of any written or oral contract, the conduct of the parties and any other circumstances (SOGA, s.17). However, sometimes buyers and sellers are not as careful as they should be and do not expressly state when they intend the property to pass, and in the absence of any other expressed intention, SOGA, s.18 has set up five rules which may be used to establish the intention of the parties. These are as follows:

(1) Where there is an unconditional contract for the sale of specific goods in a deliverable state, the property passes to the buyer when the contract is made, irrespective of any delay in the time of payment or delivery.

(2) Where there is a contract for the sale of specific goods and the seller has yet to put the goods into a deliverable state, the property does not pass until the goods are in a deliverable state and the buyer has been informed of the fact.

(3) Where there is a contract for the sale of specific goods in a deliverable state but the goods need to be measured in order to ascertain the price, the property does not pass until the measurement has taken place and the buyer has been informed of the fact.

(4)   When goods are supplied on approval or on sale or return the property passes when the buyer tells the seller of his approval (or by another action adopts the sale). However, if the buyer does not signify his approval or acceptance but retains the goods without notice of rejection beyond any specified period for rejection, the property will pass at the end of that period. If there is no specified period, the property will pass after the expiry of a reasonable time. The sort of action that presupposes acceptance is using the goods as security for some other transaction or hiring the goods to another person. It should be explained that this rule is unconnected with "inertia selling", the practice of sending unsolicited goods and subsequently intimidating unwilling recipients of the goods into buying the goods. This is forbidden under the Unsolicited Goods and Services Act 1971.

(5)   Where there is a contract for the sale of unascertained or future goods by description, and where goods of that description and in a deliverable state are "unconditionally appropriated" to the contract (*i.e.* irrevocably set aside for the contract without there being any outstanding conditions which have first to be fulfilled) by the seller with the buyer's agreement, or by the buyer with the seller's assent, the property in the goods passes to the buyer when the goods are appropriated (rule 5(1)). The assent may be done expressly or by implication (*i.e.* through the actions of the parties) and may take place either before, at or after the appropriation. Unconditional appropriation may also take place where the seller delivers the goods to the buyer or to someone on the buyer's behalf such as a carrier without reserving to himself the right to dispose of the goods (rule 5(2)). Where there is a contract for the sale of a specified quantity of unascertained goods in a deliverable state which forms part of a bulk agreed upon by the parties, and where for some reason the bulk is reduced from its original quantity but the buyer is the only remaining person due to receive goods from that bulk, the remaining quantity of the goods is to be taken as appropriated to the contract and the property therein passes to the buyer (rule 5(3)). This rule arose out of problems in the delivery of various commodities, especially where the seller had gone into liquidation. It effectively allows the goods to be ascertained by exhaustion, by taking what is remaining after other persons have taken from the bulk what is due to them even though no actual act of ascertainment by the buyer has taken place.

These five rules apply where there is no contrary indication in the contract. But there is nothing to prevent the seller retaining a right of disposal until the fulfilment of some condition (SOGA, s.19). A common example of this is a retention of title clause in a contract for the supply of goods, retaining the property in the goods with the seller until all sums due by the buyer to the seller are paid—even though the buyer may be in possession of the goods. Under SOGA, s.25(1) if the buyer disregards the retention of title clause and sells the goods anyway, any sub-buyer buying the goods in good faith and without notice of the retention of title clause is entitled to keep the goods and cannot be compelled to return them (*Archivent Sales and Development Ltd v Strathclyde Regional Council* (1985), discussed later).

When does risk pass?

Unless there is some agreement to the contrary, the normal rule is that the risk in the goods remains with the seller until the property is transferred to the buyer, irrespective of the date of delivery to the buyer (SOGA, s.20(1)). In *Pignataro v Gilroy* (1919), the buyer acquired bags of rice but failed to uplift them from the seller's premises. When the bags were stolen from those premises the buyer had to bear the loss. Consequently, as a matter of practice it is prudent always in any contract to clarify when risk passes, who will have the benefit of any insurance over the goods and who is paying the insurance premiums.

As exceptions to the general rule above, if there has been any delay in the delivery of the goods, and the delay is attributable to one of the parties to the contract, the goods are at the risk of the party at fault to the extent of the loss which arose as a result of the fault (SOGA, s.20(2)), and secondly, sellers and buyers acting as custodiers or carriers cannot rely on the above general rule to avoid the duty to take adequate care of the goods while goods are in their care or in transit (SOGA, s.20(3)).

If, however, the sale is a consumer contract, the goods remain at the seller's risk until they are delivered to the consumer (SOGA s.20(4)).

Transfer of title

If someone obtains goods which he does not own, and sells those goods without the authority or consent of the owner, the buyer gets no better title than the person purporting to sell the goods (SOGA, s.21(1)), also known by the Latin phrase *nemo dat quod non habet* (no one can give what he does not own). So if a thief sells stolen goods, the buyer may be required to hand the goods back to the true owner and sue (if he can) the thief for the value of the goods that he had to relinquish. This rule is disapplied where the owner's own conduct prevents him from objecting to the seller's right to sell the goods (SOGA, s.21(1)). This is known in Scotland as personal bar (in England, estoppel) and very rarely happens in practice, except perhaps where an owner has permitted his agent to sell the owner's goods and then changes his mind. This rule is also disapplied where goods are being sold following an attachment or other court order, or where agents are acting on the owner's behalf even though the owner had withdrawn his authority (SOGA, s.21(2)).

Where the seller of goods has a voidable title (*i.e.* a title that could be challenged, as when a seller sells goods obtained by fraud) but that title has not been reduced at the time he sells the goods to a buyer, the seller may transfer title to the goods to a buyer who buys in good faith and without notice of the seller's defect in title (SOGA, s.23). This arose in

Macleod v Kerr (1965), where Kerr sold his car to a rogue named Galloway who paid for the car with a stolen cheque. Galloway promptly sold the car to Macleod and in the meantime Galloway's cheque was dishonoured. Kerr sued Macleod to get his car back, but it was held that Kerr had failed to take sufficient steps quickly enough to reduce Galloway's voidable title. Kerr had informed the police but had not told Galloway of his fraud. His only remedy was to sue Galloway, and Macleod was able to retain the car. The significance of this case is that the unfortunate Kerr ought, in theory, to have communicated more quickly with Galloway (who was no doubt keeping well out of the way) in order to reduce the contract between Galloway and Kerr. The other significant feature is that section 23 only applies in the context of a voidable title. Where the contract is void from the beginning, because, for example, there is error in the identity of the buyer (as in *Morrison v Robertson* (1908)), section 23 does not apply and the original owner will be able to retrieve his goods from the person possessing the goods.

In the context of hire purchase, where a purported seller of a motor vehicle being acquired by the seller under a hire purchase agreement sells that vehicle, a buyer (other than a car dealer) buying it in good faith without notice of the finance company's interest in the vehicle may obtain good title to the vehicle (Hire-Purchase Act 1964, s.27(1),(2)). The exception relating to car dealers arises from the perception that car dealers are well able to look after their own interests without the extra benefit of consumer protection.

Where a seller has sold goods to a buyer and received payment for the goods, but the goods are in the possession of the seller, if the seller inadvertently or fraudulently transfers or delivers the goods to a new buyer buying in good faith and without knowledge of the fact that the goods belong to the first buyer, the new buyer gets good title to the goods (SOGA, s.24). The first buyer is then entitled to sue the seller for damages for non-delivery. Where a seller delivers goods to a buyer who then delivers or transfers the goods to a sub-buyer who buys the goods in good faith and without notice of any rights of the original seller, the sub-buyer obtains good title to the goods (SOGA, s.25(1)). In *Archivent Sales and Development Ltd v Strathclyde Regional Council* (1985), the seller delivered goods to a contractor carrying out work at a school. The contractor sold on the goods to the school, despite not having paid the original seller who had attempted to safeguard his position with a retention of title clause. As the goods had been transferred to the school's owners, who had acquired the goods in good faith and without knowledge of the rights of the original seller, the seller was unable to assert his claim to the goods. Accordingly section 25(1) limits the applicability of retention of title clauses. This rule does not, however, apply in the context of conditional sale agreements regulated under the Consumer Credit Act 1974, s.25 or in the context of acquisitions by car dealers (as referred to above).

How is the contract of sale to be carried out?

It is the duty of the seller to deliver the goods and the duty of the buyer to accept the goods and to pay for them, all in accordance with the terms of the contract for the sale of the goods (SOGA, s.27). Unless the contract says otherwise, delivery and payment are concurrent, and both parties should be ready to perform their parts of the contract simultaneously. There are varied and pragmatic rules to govern such matters as where delivery is to take place (SOGA, s.29), the delivery of more or less goods than had been requested (SOGA, s.30) (more of the required quantity entitles the buyer to reject the excess, very much more entitles the buyer to reject it all; if too little is delivered, the buyer must pay at the contracted rate for what he receives and claim damages for non-performance of the rest of the contract, while delivery of far too little entitles the buyer to reject it all), delivery by instalments (SOGA, s.32) and delivery to carriers, where generally delivery to the carrier is deemed to be delivery to the buyer; but in each of these events the precise details may be varied by agreement between the parties, and if the buyer is a consumer, delivery of the goods to the carrier is not delivery of the goods to the buyer (SOGA s.32(4)). Where the seller delivers goods to the buyer, the buyer must be allowed a reasonable time to examine the goods to see if they conform to the contract or to see if the bulk of the goods matches previously seen samples (SOGA, s.34). He is not held to have accepted the goods until he has been afforded these opportunities for examination even if he has signed an acceptance receipt (SOGA, s.35(2)). In a consumer contract, a consumer is not deprived of this right even if apparently made to do so by the terms of his contract (SOGA, s.35(3)). The buyer is held to have accepted the goods where he tells the seller he has done so (SOGA, s.35(1)(a)), or where he treats the goods in a manner which is inconsistent with the ownership of the seller, for example, where he uses them as security for some other transaction. Subject to the next paragraph, if a buyer retains the goods for a reasonable time without telling the seller that he is rejecting them, he is deemed to have accepted the goods (SOGA, s.35(4)). If the buyer asks the seller to repair the goods, the request does not signify acceptance (SOGA, s.35 (6)(a)); and even if the goods are delivered to someone else through a subsale the buyer may still be entitled to reject the goods within a reasonable time (SOGA, s.35(6)(b)). Where the goods are units within a bigger and ultimately indivisible set of goods, as, for example, one print within a narrative series of prints all within a limited edition, the acceptance of the one item is deemed to be an acceptance of all the items (SOGA, s.35(7)).

The buyer's right of rejection and other rights

The buyer may if necessary reject the goods, except where he has accepted the goods in the circumstances outlined in the previous paragraph, or where the breach by the seller of a term of the contract is not sufficiently material to entitle the buyer to reject the goods (SOGA, s.15B). Accordingly, if the courts decide in a case that the time for rejection of delivered goods is past, but the goods are still not to the buyer's satisfaction in terms of quality, the buyer's remaining remedy, assuming the claim is justified, is damages arising out of the loss directly and naturally resulting from the breach of the contract in terms of quality (SOGA, s.53A). It is sometimes possible both to claim damages and to reject the goods (SOGA, s.15B). Unless the terms of the contract say otherwise, it is possible to have partial rejection, where the buyer is entitled to reject all of an entire consignment of goods but instead chooses to keep the satisfactory goods and reject the unsatisfactory goods (SOGA, s.35A). This rule applies both in respect of a single delivery or delivery by instalments. Formerly it was only possible to reject all the goods or none of them. If a buyer legitimately rejects goods, he is not bound to return them to the seller unless the terms of the contract of sale say otherwise. He must, however, intimate his rejection to the seller (SOGA, s.36). If the buyer after a reasonable time delays or refuses to accept the goods when he should properly do so, the buyer is liable to the seller for the cost of storage and care of the goods (SOGA, s.37). Following the implementation of the Sale and Supply of Goods Regulations 2002 ("SSGR") if the buyer is a consumer, the time for rejection is now up to six months from the period of delivery, thus significantly benefiting consumers who formerly had to report any defects swiftly after purchase (SOGA, s.48A(3)). Under SOGA, s.48B the buyer may require the seller to repair the goods if they are faulty, or to replace them within a reasonable time and with minimal inconvenience and expense to the buyer. As a further option, the buyer can insist on the price being lowered instead (SOGA, s.48C). These remedies are subject to safeguards for the seller to allow him reasonable time to effect repairs or replacements (SOGA, s.48D), or to allow him to prove that the goods were conform to requirements in the first place (SOGA, s.48A(3)).

Other rights for the buyer

Where the seller neglects or refuses to deliver the goods to the buyer, the buyer may claim damages for non-delivery (SOGA, s.51). Equally, in the case of a contract of sale of specific or ascertained goods, the buyer may raise an action of specific implement to enforce delivery of the goods (SOGA, s.52). This means that the court pronounces an order compelling the seller to perform his part of the contract.

If a seller has provided a guarantee either from himself or the manufacturer, the guarantee must be in plain intelligible English and comes into effect at the time of delivery of the goods. It also allows the consumer to sue the manufacturer directly without involving the retailer (SSGR, reg.15).

The seller's rights

Where a seller has not been paid (known as the "unpaid seller") he is entitled to retain the goods until payment while he possesses the goods, even if the property in the goods has transferred to the buyer, and in the event of the insolvency of the buyer, he may also stop any goods that are in transit to the buyer (SOGA, s.39(1)(a), (b)). Where some of the goods have been delivered by the unpaid seller to the buyer, but the remainder has not, the seller may withhold delivery of the remainder pending payment. The unpaid seller also has a right of resale (SOGA, s.39(2)), subject to intimation to the buyer giving him a reasonable time within which to make payment. These rights may be abrogated by the terms of the contract, as where an arbitration clause takes effect. Where the seller is no longer in possession of the goods or they are still in transit to the buyer as above, he may raise an action for the price (SOGA, s.49(1)), or claim damages for non-acceptance where the buyer ought properly to have accepted and paid for the goods (SOGA, s.50).

DELICTUAL LIABILITY

Problems with SOGA, s.14 and the duty of care

If a seller sells goods whose defects cause damage to the buyer, the seller incurs strict liability under SOGA, s.14. However, under SOGA only the buyer may sue only the seller for the goods' defects, as opposed to suing the manufacturer (who may be better placed to meet any claim). So if a buyer bought goods as a present for his uncle, his uncle could not sue the seller for any injury caused to him by the goods. What the buyer can sue for is the estimated loss directly and naturally arising in the ordinary course of events from the breach (SOGA, s.53A) and any consequential losses where those cause damage to the buyer personally or to his property—but not to the uncle or his property.

Accordingly where injured non-buyers wish to raise an action against a seller, or where an injured buyer or non-buyer wishes to raise an action against the manufacturer, he may make a claim for negligence arising out of a breach of the manufacturer's general duty of care, as in *Donoghue v Stevenson* (1932). Alternatively, where a victim suffers injury from defective components in manufactured goods, he may raise an action against the producer of the goods under the Consumer Protection Act 1987 ("CPA"), which provides for strict liability for defective products. This Act is derived from the E.C. Product Liability Directive 85/374 and serves to some extent to provide a remedy for victims of defective products produced by a producer (commonly a manufacturer, but the term "producer" can also mean retailer if it is not apparent who the manufacturer is (CPA, s.2 and see next paragraph)). Victims making a claim still have to overcome the hurdles imposed by the permissible defences open to producers under CPA, s.4. It is not possible for the producer to contract out of the strict liability provisions (CPA, s.7) though it is possible for a victim to be contributorily negligent whereupon any damages payable by the producer will be abated to the extent of the victim's own negligence (CPA, s.4, referring to the Law Reform (Contributory Negligence) Act 1945 and the Fatal Accidents Act 1976, s.5).

The liability of producers
Producers may try to evade liability by claiming that they were not the manufacturers of a harmful product. Accordingly producers, if they are not the manufacturers themselves, may be held liable where they unreasonably delay or refuse to identify who the true producer is (CPA, s.2(3)), although this rule does not apply where goods are supplied other than in the course of a business, in order to protect the parties in private transactions (CPA, s.4(1)(c)). Businesses that produce their "own brand" products, such as supermarkets, are treated as if they were producers themselves unless they make it clear who the actual manufacturer is (CPA, s.2(2)(b)). Importers bringing in goods from outside the European Union are treated as constructive producers (CPA, s.2(2)(c)). The word "product" does not include buildings though it does include items fitted into buildings, so that, say, a defective heating system that gassed a consumer could give rise to compensation (CPA, s.46). There is no requirement to prove that a producer is negligent in order to assert a claim: it is enough to prove that the product was defective, *i.e.* that its safety is not such as persons generally are entitled to expect (CPA, s.3(1)), and safety in this context applies to property as well as to personal injury or death (CPA, s.3(1)). However, the victim still has to prove the damage, the defect in the product and the causal relationship between the two.

Protection for the manufacturer and the "state of the art" defence
When this Act was under consideration it was recognised that too strict an application of the principle for the requirement of safety could lead to a stifling of inventive talent, and so there are safeguards in CPA, s.4 to protect the producer:

(a) where the goods are manufactured in compliance with E.C. safety rules;
(b) where the products were used without the producer's authority (as when the products have been stolen);
(c) where the products have not been supplied in a commercial transaction;
(d) where the fault is attributable to some other producer's misuse of the products;
(e) where the fault lies in the overall design which is not of the producer's making ;
(f) where the defect did not exist in the product at the relevant time;
(g) where the state of the art defence applies.

The most significant safeguard is the "state of the art" defence in CPA, s.4(1)(e): that the defect was such that given the state of scientific and technical knowledge at the time, a similar producer of similar products would also have been unaware of the defect. This is an objective test and the producer's own knowledge of other businesses or of scientific and technical matters is not enough: the producer, irrespective of his own resources, is expected to be aware of the most recent developments in the area of the product and cannot rely on his own ignorance. Nevertheless it is a significant protective measure for producers and correspondingly a significant hurdle for victims making a claim.

Prohibition on small claims and on claims for pure economic loss

Under CPA damages are available for personal injury or damage to property (including land), though to discourage small claims, only claims where the damages would amount to more than £275 will be entertained by the court (CPA, s.5(4)). CPA, s.5 prohibits claims for pure economic loss, so that if, say, a component in a lawnmower breaks down, the pursuer can neither claim for the faulty component in the lawnmower nor for the cost of the repair to the lawnmower as a whole (CPA, s.5(2)). However, if the component in the lawnmower caused injury to the owner or to somebody else or to other property, that damage would be an allowable claim. Where damage is caused by a faulty component added at a later date to the lawnmower, but which was not originally part of the lawnmower, it is possible to claim for the damage to the lawnmower as a result of the faulty component (since it is now treated as "property"), though it is not possible to claim for the value of the actual component itself. This is because the claim for the actual component could be made under SOGA, s.14. CPA serves to provide a remedy of damages arising out of physical injury to people or damage to property but is not concerned with obtaining damages which could be used to pay for the cost of the faulty component itself. Claims under the CPA may be made only up to ten years after the product was supplied, and within three years of the later of the date of the injury or damage (subject to certain exceptions) (CPA, Sch.2, amending the Prescription and Limitation (Scotland) Act 1973).

CRIMINAL LIABILITY

In addition to the civil law protection for the consumer outlined above, there is a large body of criminal law designed to protect the consumer. The main Acts dealing with this matter are the Trade Descriptions Act 1968 and Parts II and III of the CPA, though there are many others which have an important part to play such as the Weights and Measures Act 1965, the Financial Services Act 1986 and specifically for estate agents' benefit, the Property Misdescriptions Act 1991. Errant producers, sellers or agents, as the case may be, may suffer criminal penalties for breaches of the legislation.

The Trades Descriptions Act 1968 ("TDA")

This act prohibits false trade descriptions (TDA, s.1) which are false to a material degree (TDA, s.3(1)) or, where not false, are misleading (TDA, s.3(2)). A false description need not be in writing: an oral representation is sufficient (TDA, s.4(2)) and applies equally to advertisements as to the actual goods (TDA, s.6). TDA does not just apply to goods; it applies also to services (TDA, s.14). There are criminal sanctions for any offences contravening the TDA which can apply both to individuals and to the company employing those individuals (TDA, s.20). There are defences to TDA if it can be proved that the accused was mistaken as the result of someone else's fault (TDA, s.24(1)(a)) and that it was reasonable for him to rely on that other person, providing that other person has been identified to the court (TDA, s.24(2)), or that the mistake was a matter otherwise beyond the accused's control. There is also a defence of "due diligence" open to the accused where he has been prosecuted for breach of the legislation (TDA, s.24(1)(b)): due diligence requires that the fault lies not with the accused but with some other person who failed to pass on the relevant information or to carry out some required act, and that the accused "took all reasonable precautions and exercised all due diligence" (*i.e.* did all that could reasonably be expected of him) to prevent the fault occurring. It is therefore wise for businesses to set up proper training methods and procedures to ensure that misleading advertisements do not occur. Advertising agents and newspapers printing other people's advertisements are not liable for misleading advertisements providing that they had no reason to suspect their publication would lead to an offence under TDA (TDA, s.25). The local Weights and Measures Inspectorate and Trading Standards Authorities ("TSA") have powers to enter premises and make test purchases to ensure proper compliance with TDA. However, if the officers of the Inspectorate or the TSA seize goods or other items which are subsequently found not to have contravened the requirements of TDA, the Inspectorate or TSA must compensate the goods' owner for any loss that he suffers.

Consumer safety under CPA, Part II

Producers' breaches of consumer safety may result in prosecution (CPA, s.10). Under the CPA it is a defence to prosecution for breach of consumer safety requirements to state that the accused reasonably believed that the goods were not being used or consumed in the United Kingdom, or that at the time of offering the goods for sale in the course of his business as a retail trader he neither knew, nor had reasonable grounds for believing, that the goods failed to comply with the safety requirement, or that he did not offer the goods as new and that those buying the goods intended to buy the goods in their imperfect state (CPA, s.10(4)). The Secretary of State has power to make regulations to provide for consumer safety and this is normally done in consultation with retail organisations, manufacturers and the Health and Safety Commission (CPA, s.11(5)). Adherence to these regulations is naturally advantageous to the accused facing prosecution (CPA, s.10(3)). Under such regulations there may be, initially, prohibitory notices and warning notices in order to dissuade the producer or seller from selling the unsafe goods (CPA, s.13), but if these are insufficient, suspension notices may be served on anyone selling goods which may be in breach of the safety regulations (CPA, s.14). Where the enforcement authority has made a mistake and there is no contravention the enforcement authority is required to compensate the supplier of the goods (CPA, s.14(7)). It is open to the relevant authorities to seize and forfeit the accused's goods where they fail to comply with the required standards (CPA, s.17).

Misleading price indications under CPA, Part III

Under Part III of the CPA, it is a criminal offence for a person to give misleading information to consumers about the prices at which goods, services, accommodation or other facilities may be available (CPA, s.20(1)). As "misleading" is inherently an uncertain word, section 21 indicates that a price indication is misleading if it fails to state what a consumer might reasonably expect it to cover, if it suggests that the price is less than it actually is, if it fails to include additional charges or if it fails to detail facts or circumstances which have a bearing on the price, thus ensuring that it is difficult for the consumer to compare prices. Part III extends to the provision of services, including banking, insurance, foreign currency transactions, electricity, parking and caravan residence (CPA, s.22). CPA does not, however, apply to contracts of employment, investment services or the sale of new homes (CPA, s.23). There are defences to Part III: that the accused has complied with non-statutory codes of practices in the relevant industry (such codes having been drawn up in conjunction with the Secretary of State and/or the Director of Fair Trading (CPA, s.25(2))); that the information is contained in newspaper articles, as opposed to advertisements within newspapers, and is not actionable under the CPA (CPA, s.24(2)); that publishers of advertisements in newspapers are not liable if they did not know and had no grounds for suspecting that the advertisements were misleading (CPA, s.24(3)); that the indication as to prices for goods, services, accommodation or facilities did not relate to the availability from the accused of any of those goods and services, etc., as the accused had merely been recommending a price at which the providers of those goods and services, etc. could offer them, that price being reasonable under the circumstances—even if some providers chose not to follow that price so that it appeared to be a misleading price (CPA, s.24(4)). The accused may also use the due diligence defence in a similar manner to the one referred to above (CPA, s.39).

As with the TDA, there are provisions for enforcement by authorised officers of the relevant bodies (CPA, s.27), enabling the officers to make test purchases (CPA, s.28), search and seize goods and papers (CPA, s.29) but also to pay compensation where they have failed to obtain a conviction (CPA, s.34).

Further reading

Cusine and Forte, *Scottish Cases in Commercial Law* (2nd ed., Butterworths, 1998).
Ervine, *Consumer Law in Scotland* (2nd ed., W. Green, 2000).
Forte (ed.), *Scots Commercial Law* (Butterworths, 1997), Chap.2.
Gloag and Henderson, *The Laws of Scotland* (11th ed., 2001), Chaps 16 and 17.
Mays (ed.), *Scots Law: A Student Guide* (T&T Clark, 2000), 8–62 to 8–105.
Thomas and Ervine, *Encyclopaedia of Consumer Law* (Sweet & Maxwell, looseleaf updated regularly).

2. HIRE OF GOODS

A hire of goods differs from a sale of goods in that during a hire the owner (known during the hire as the lessor) retains ownership of the goods and the hirer merely has the use or possession of the goods. At the end of the period of hire possession reverts to the owner. The law relating to hire is mostly covered by the common law and by the Supply of Goods and Services Act 1982 ("SGSA"), the Consumer Credit Act 1974 ("CCA"), the Unfair Contract Terms Act 1977 ("UCTA") and the Unfair Terms in Consumer Contracts Regulations 1999 ("UTCCR").

Regulated hire agreements
While the common law regulates contracts of hire generally, a hire agreement involving a consumer (which term denotes ordinary consumers, sole traders and partnerships but not limited companies or limited liability partnerships (CCA, s.189(1))), enduring for more than three months, and requiring the consumer/hirer to make payments amounting to less than £25,000 in value, is known as a *regulated hire agreement* (CCA, s.15). This means that the hirer is entitled to the protection of CCA. Consequently the terms of the hire must be properly and clearly set out on appropriately designed forms (CCA, s.60) which in turn must be properly drawn up and executed in accordance with the regulations of CCA (CCA, s.61). All regulated hire agreements must be in writing, with copies made available to the hirer (CCA, s.63), clearly explaining both parties' rights. Failure to follow the correct procedure and wordings on all documentation may invalidate the hire or delay the enforcement of the lessor's rights of repossession by requiring the lessor to apply to the court (CCA, s.65). This is to protect the hirer from the sudden and possibly arbitrary repossession of the hired goods and from the requirement to make unexpected termination payments or pay other

penalties of which the hirer may have been unaware. There is judicial control of any such attempts at repossession by the use of time orders, giving the hirer time to pay, or even reducing or discharging the sum the hirer is due to pay, all on the principle of fairness to the consumer (CCA, ss.126–136). Prior to the hire, the hirer is entitled to cancel the agreement during a cooling off period of five days if there have been face to face negotiations prior to the signing of the hire agreement and if the hire agreement has been signed somewhere other than at the lessor's (or his agent's) premises (CCA, s.68); following cancellation the goods must be returned to the lessor and any hire payments returned to the hirer (CCA, ss.67–72). There are detailed rules to deal with default by the hirer, requiring notices to be sent to the hirer explaining his default and giving him the opportunity to remedy it (CCA, ss. 87–89) and other rules to cover early repayment (CCA, ss. 94–97) and the termination of the agreement (CCA, ss. 98–104).

Hire agreements which are not regulated hire agreements are covered by SGSA (see next paragraph) and by the terms of the hire agreement itself, on the grounds that those who can afford to deal in sums greater than £25,000 ought to be able to look after their financial affairs without the State having to help them. Similarly limited companies and limited liability partnerships entering into hire agreements already receive some protection by virtue of their members' limited liability and should not be entitled to any more protection.

The effect of the Supply of Goods and Services Act 1982
Broadly speaking, SGSA implies into contracts of hire, including regulated hire agreements, many of the same terms that are applied to contracts of sale under SOGA (as detailed in the previous Chapter), so that there are implied terms that the hirer has title to lease the goods (SGSA, s.11H(1)(a)) and that the hirer may enjoy quiet possession of the goods (SGSA, s.11H(2)). As with SOGA, there are rules to ensure that goods hired on the basis of a description conform to that description (SGSA, s.11I), that goods hired on the basis sample conform to the bulk (SGSA, s.11K), and that the goods are of satisfactory quality and fit for their purpose (SGSA, s.11J).

The liability of the lessor
It is expected that the hired goods will be serviceable for the duration of the hire, but if repairs are necessary these should be at the lessor's expense, except where the hire agreement says otherwise or where the repairs are necessary because of the hirer's fault. Where the hired goods cause damage to people or property, the lessor is strictly liable under the Consumer Protection Act 1987 in the same manner as a supplier under a contract of sale (see previous Chapter at pp. 17-18). He also can suffer the same civil and/or criminal penalties as a supplier should the hired goods derogate from the required standard of safety that can be expected. The lessor cannot contract out of the provisions of UCTA relating to the

lessor's liability for personal injury or death arising out of the hired goods (UCTA, s.16(1)(a)), and any other exclusion clauses will only be acceptable where they are "fair and reasonable" (UCTA, s.16(1)(b)). Any consumer hire agreement on standard terms which has not been individually negotiated with the hirer may be set aside by the courts (in the same manner as contracts of sale) if the contract is significantly one-sided in favour of the non-consumer party to the contract (*i.e.* the lessor) and if there is an element of lack of good faith (UCTTR, reg.4.1).

The liability of the hirer

The hirer must pay his hire charges as contracted or, in the absence of a specified rate, at a reasonable rate. In a regulated hire agreement the rates in any event would have to be properly detailed. If the goods are faulty the hirer is normally entitled to deduct a reasonable sum to reflect his inability to use the hired goods satisfactorily. The hirer is under a duty of care to look after the goods properly in the manner that a prudent and sensible person would look after his own property. He would not be responsible for fair wear and tear, but he would be responsible if he wore the goods out through overwork or overuse (Bell's *Principles*, §141).

Further reading

Forte (ed.), *Scots Commercial Law* (Butterworths, 1997), Chap.2.

Gloag and Henderson, *The Law of Scotland* (11th ed., W. Green, 2001), Chap.24.

Mays (ed.), *Scots Law: A Student Guide* (T & T Clark, 2000) 8–106 to 8–111.

3. CONSUMER CREDIT

The purpose of the legislation

The Consumer Credit Act 1974 ("CCA") was introduced in order to: (a) provide a new, rational and coherent set of rules regulating the provision of credit; (b) set up a licensing system so that only authorised credit dealers could provide credit; and (c) set out a framework for the proper and fair provision of credit.

The aspects of CCA that deal with hire (as opposed to hire purchase) are dealt with in Chapter 2.

Licensing requirements

Under CCA, s.21 only licensed traders, lenders or credit brokers may carry on the business of consumer credit and consumer hire. Under CCA, s.147 only licensees may carry out the business of credit brokerage, debt-adjustment, debt-counselling, debt-collecting or the operation of credit reference agencies (known collectively as ancillary credit business). However, an occasional or "one-off" loan, made by someone not in the course of a business, does not normally require the credit-provider or arranger to be licensed (CCA, s.189(2)) and certain bodies such as local authorities are exempt from the licence requirement (CCA, s.21(2)). There are two types of licence, these being a "standard" licence (the more usual) and a "group" licence (CCA, s.22(1)). All businesses carrying on licensable credit business, other than those operating through group licences, such as solicitors under the aegis of the Law Society of Scotland, must obtain a standard licence, and each company within a group, as with a bank and its subsidiaries, must obtain a separate standard licence. Licences will only be issued if the Director General of Fair Trading, who supervises the operation of CCA, is satisfied that the licensee is fit to hold a licence. His criteria take into account not only the licencee's business name (lest there be any confusion with any other business of a similar name and nature), but also its compliance and its employees' compliance with the requirements of CCA (CCA, s.25). There is a public register of licensees, and penalties for carrying on a licensable credit business without a suitable licence (CCA, ss.39 and 147).

THE PROTECTION AFFORDED TO THE CONSUMER

Who is a "consumer"?

In the context of the CCA, a consumer is an individual wishing to enter a credit arrangement of less than £25,000 (CCA, s.8(2)). Individuals in this context means private persons, partnerships of private persons, unincorporated clubs, charities and societies (CCA, s.189(1)). Incorporated bodies such as limited companies do not count as individuals except in the context of a joint hire to an individual and a limited company under CCA, s.185(5).

The meaning of "credit"?

Credit is a cash loan and any other form of financial accommodation, cash here meaning money in any form (CCA, s.9(1)). The wording is deliberately wide so that most forms of credit will be caught by the legislation—in the interests of the consumer.

REGULATED AGREEMENTS

Regulated agreements are any agreements that are regulated by CCA, of which the most common are described below. Under CCA, s.16 and the

Consumer Credit (Exempt Agreements) Order 1989 (SI 1989/869)("CC(EA)O"), some credit agreements are exempt from all the regulations, as explained later. It is possible to have some credit arrangements that feature several different types of arrangement, in which case they are known as multiple agreements.

Consumer credit arrangement

A personal credit arrangement is any agreement between a debtor and a creditor for credit of any amount. This is to be contrasted with a (regulated) consumer credit arrangement, which is one where the consumer is an individual as defined above and the sum of credit is £25,000 or less (CCA, s.8(2)), unless it is exempt under CCA, s.16.

Hire-purchase

Hire-purchase is treated as a form of credit as, in effect, it spreads the cost of acquiring goods over a period of time by means of regular hire payments followed by an option to purchase (CCA, s.189(1)). During the period of hire and under the terms of the hire-purchase agreement the consumer is still liable for any damage and for any repairs necessary. If the consumer fails to maintain his monthly payments, the finance company is entitled to repossess the goods and sell them to defray its loss. Where the goods are repossessed, the CCA lays down careful rules to ensure that the consumer is treated fairly in respects of the payments he has already made. Hire-purchase agreements are regulated by the CCA ss.9(3), 15(1)(a). They are treated as consumer credit agreements for fixed sum credit.

Running account credit (CCA, s.10(1)(a))

This is a facility whereby the borrower may borrow up to £25,000. He may make repayments into the account and then borrow again from the account providing that at no stage is the total amount borrowed greater than £25,000.

Fixed sum credit (CCA, s.10(1)(b))

This is a less flexible arrangement than a running account credit. With fixed sum credit a sum of money is borrowed in one amount or in instalments. Both of these are extensively used by banks when offering loans to customers. They may be contrasted with overdrafts which are specifically exempt from CCA by virtue of CCA, s.74.

Restricted use agreement (CCA, s.11)

In this situation the credit may only be used for onc purpose, as opposed to an *unrestricted use agreement* which may be used for any purpose. Restricted use agreements are common in the situation of hire-purchase agreements where the credit is provided for the one use only, such as the purchase of a car. A restricted use agreement enables the creditor to

monitor the debtor's use of the credit more closely, in return for which the
creditor may be able to offer a lower interest rate.

Debtor—creditor—supplier agreement (CCA, s.12)

This is an agreement between a debtor (usually a customer), a creditor
(usually a finance company) and a supplier (often a retailer). A common
example of this is a credit card such as Visa or American Express. If a
customer buys a computer from a supplier using his credit card, he pays
for the computer with the credit facility offered by the credit card
company. The credit card company pays the supplier, and the customer
will find the cost of the computer on his next statement from the credit
card company. He has to pay the amount due on his statement plus any
interest if due. The advantage to the supplier is that it knows it will get
paid, since a cheque from the customer might not clear; the advantage to
the customer is that he can buy the computer quickly and if the supplier
defaults, the customer has a joint and several claim against both the
supplier and the credit card company, albeit that the credit card company
may then be indemnified by the supplier (CCA, s.75). This is known as
connected lender liability. This rule does not apply where the claim
relates to an item whose cash price from the supplier is less than £100 or
is greater than £30,000. The particular advantage of the CCA, s.75 is that
where the supplier goes into liquidation, the consumer can still claim
against the credit card company should he need to do so.

Credit token agreements (CCA, s. 14)

This is a regulated agreement which applies to such forms of credit as
storecards. The credit token does not need to be limited to the one outlet
(as with a storecard that only provides credit for the one shop) though that
is its common use.

Where a debtor allows someone else to use his credit token, he is liable
for any loss to the creditor arising from that use (CCA, s.84(2)), but when
the credit token is used by an unauthorised person, the debtor is liable up
to the sum of £50 to the creditor (CCA, s.84(1)). If the debtor finds his
credit token has been stolen or otherwise lost and immediately informs
the credit token provider of his loss, liability does not arise (Consumer
Credit (Credit Token Agreements) Regulations 1983).

Credit agreements exempt under CCA (CCA, s.16)

Certain credit agreements are specifically exempt from the consumer
credit legislation. These are:

(a) normal trade credit agreements (excepting hire purchase agreements,
     land purchase agreements and agreements secured by a pledge) for a
     fixed sum repayable in no more than four payments within a period
     of a year (CC(EA)O, art.3(1)(a)(i)) and for a running account credit
     agreement (subject to the same exceptions as above) repayable in

one lump sum within a designated period (CC(EA)O, art.3(1)(a)(ii))—as in a Gold Card or Diners Club card;
(b) land transactions repayable in no more than four repayments (CC(EA)O, art.3(1)(b));
(c) mortgage lending for the acquisition of land or the securing of a loan upon land (CCA, s.16(1),(2));
(d) low cost credit, where the cost of the loan is not greater than base rate plus 1 per cent or 13 per cent, whichever is the higher (CC(EA)O, art.4));
(e) loans for certain insurance policies, usually to pay the premiums on property insurance or mortgage protection policies (CC(EA)O, art.3));
(f) credit agreements for the financing of exports from or imports into the United Kingdom (CC(EA)O, art.5));
(g) consumer credit arrangements where the creditor is a housing authority and where the agreement is secured by a standard security on a house (CCA, s.16(6A)).

The hiring of gas, electricity or water meters is exempt from the legislation (CC(EA)O, art.6). All other agreements, covered by the CCA and not exempt, are "regulated agreements".

General rules for regulated agreements
CCA operates to ensure that any advertising carried out by consumer credit businesses is accurate and intelligible, complete with "health warnings" alerting the borrower or hirer to the penalties arising from non-fulfilment of his requirements (CCA, ss.43–47). The annual percentage charge for credit ("APR") must be clearly visible and include hidden charges. Quotations are similarly closely regulated (CCA, ss.52–54). Canvassing or soliciting of customers must be fairly done, and may only take place off trade premises under very restricted circumstances (CCA, ss.48–51). All agreements regulated by CCA have to follow certain specified forms and procedures (CCA, ss.60–66), one of which is a "cooling-off" period during which time the debtor may change his mind (CCA, s.68). The debtor is permitted to cancel an agreement within five days of either receiving a copy of the executed agreement (where it was signed off trade premises (CCA, s.67(a)) or the date when he received notice of the debtor's rights of cancellation intimated to him under CCA, s.64.

Notwithstanding the above, CCA, s.74 excludes four types of agreement from the above rules, these being:

(a) non-commercial agreements (*i.e.* one-off non-business loans);
(b) current account overdrafts;
(c) loans in connection with debts due after a death (such as a loan by a bank to pay inheritance tax due by the deceased's estate); and

(d) small agreements for restricted use credit for the provision of credit
     of less than £50.

With all regulated agreements (other than those exempted by CCA,
s.74), the creditor may not enforce his rights unless he has notified the
debtor of his intention to do so by means of a default notice (CCA, s.87).
In the process of enforcing his rights, or should the debtor choose to
object to the enforcement, the matter may come before the courts, which
may grant a time order for payment (CCA, s.129) or in the case of hire
purchase, a return order or a transfer order (CCA, s.133). This will
normally be a method of allowing the debtor time to pay off this debts by
instalments or to remedy any breach (CCA, s.129). Any lapse by the
creditor in the provision of all the necessary forms and documentation for
the agreement may make the creditor's application for enforcement
invalid, or delay it until the documentation is correct. Anybody granting
security or a guarantee as part of any credit transaction will also need to
be given the appropriate documentation to ensure that he is aware of the
implication of his grant of security (CCA, ss.105–113).

Under CCA, ss.98–104 termination of regulated agreements may only
be done in accordance with the strict provisions of the Act.

Pawnbroking

Strict rules apply to pawnbrokers and their documentation with regard to
the pawning of goods. The pawnbroker must give each customer a copy
of the pawn agreement, a notice of his cancellation rights and a receipt for
the pawned goods (CCA, s.114). The pawn will be redeemable within a
period of six months or such longer period as may be agreed (CCA,
s.116) or the goods will pass to the pawnbroker who may sell the goods
after intimation to the customer (CCA, s.121). If after the sale of the
goods there is a surplus after repayment of the loan and interest and
expenses, the surplus is repayable to the customer (CCA, s.121(3)). If the
sale proceeds are less than the sum due, the balance remains outstanding
from the customer to the pawnbroker (CCA, s.121(4)).

Extortionate credit transactions

An extortionate credit transaction is a credit transaction which the court
decides is extortionate. The court, at its discretion, may rewrite the
transaction so that a fairer contract subsists. Grounds for deeming a credit
transaction extortionate would be unreasonable rates of interest, the
borrower's current financial pressures and any other relevant facts about
the borrower. If a borrower alleges that the transaction is extortionate, it is
for the creditor to prove that it is not (CCA, s.171(7)).

Further reading

Thomas and Ervine, *Encyclopaedia of Consumer Law* (Sweet & Maxwell,
    looseleaf updated regularly).

Ervine, *Consumer Law in Scotland* (2nd ed., W. Green, 2000), Chap.9.
Gloag and Henderson, *The Law of Scotland* (11th ed., W. Green, 2001),
    Chap.18.
Goode, *Consumer Credit, Law and Practice* (Butterworths).

---

4. CAUTION AND GUARANTEES

Caution (pronounced "kay-shun") is the Scots legal term for a guarantee.
The term is now falling into disuse except in the context of "lodging
caution" which is where the court orders that a party to a court action
lodges funds, either in the form of cash or an insurance policy (sometimes
known as a "bond of caution") to cover his opponent's costs. As the
requirement to lodge caution can give rise to injustice for impoverished
litigants, the courts do not lightly use this power.

The more common term for caution nowadays is a guarantee. With a
guarantee there must be a debtor who is due money or required to fulfil
some other obligation ("the principal debt") for a creditor, who in turn
seeks reassurance by way of guarantee from the guarantor that if the
debtor defaults, the guarantor will make good any loss to the creditor. The
guarantee is ancillary to the principal debt, so that if the debt is
extinguished, so too is the guarantee.

A guarantee is a *ius in personam* (right against a person) and therefore
gives the creditor no better rights in the guarantor's assets than any other
creditor in the event of the guarantor's insolvency.

The common uses of guarantees
Guarantees are commonly required: (a) by banks as a form of security
from directors personally or a holding company where a new and/or
subsidiary company wants to borrow money; (b) by banks on the occasion
of the opening of a new bank account for, or a loan to a possibly
unreliable customer; (c) in the form of performance bonds, to ensure the
completion of a project in the event of the insolvency of the contractor.

The form of the guarantee
It may be unwise not to have a guarantee in writing but it is not illegal: it
merely leads to problems of proof. However, where a guarantee is
gratuitous and is not given in the course of business, it must be in writing
(Requirements of Writing (Scotland)Act 1995, s.1(2)(ii)). Otherwise it
may be in writing, or may be evidenced by actings or parole evidence.

There is no standard wording for guarantees, though most bank
guarantees will normally state the extent of the guarantor's liability, his
requirement to pay any interest and expenses and the duration of the
guarantee. Commonly there will be a clause giving warrant for

preservation and execution, thus enabling the bank to effect summary (*i.e.* immediate) diligence against the guarantor. Prudent guarantors will insist on only being liable for a fixed sum, or a fixed proportion of the total sum and no more (known as "benefit of division") as opposed to being jointly and severally liable. They will also wish to ensure that the guarantee relates only to a specific transaction as opposed to all of the debtor's transactions generally. Prescription applies to guarantees, and after five years the liability under the guarantee prescribes (Prescription and Limitation (Scotland) Act 1973, s.6).

Guarantees for a spouse's debts

Following the important case of *Royal Bank of Scotland v Etridge* (2002), if a bank (or other creditor) wishes the spouse of a debtor to guarantee a loan or other facility for the debtor's business debts, the bank is put on enquiry and must ensure that the spouse takes independent legal advice before he or she signs the guarantee. The bank must furnish the spouse's solicitor with the financial information relating to the debtor's loan, so that the full implications of the spouse's liability under the guarantee may be explained by the solicitor to the spouse. The bank must receive evidence from the spouse's solicitor that the advice has been given and that the spouse consented to the solicitor's provision of that evidence to the bank. The solicitor in so doing acts as the agent of the spouse and not of the lender, and the bank is entitled to assume that the solicitor will act properly. This procedure should ensure that the spouse becomes fully aware of what he or she is accepting. The procedure also protects the bank because (a) in the past some guarantees were void because over-trusting spouses had been co-erced by debtors into signing guarantees without appreciating their significance, and therefore had not truly consented to the provision of the guarantee, and (b) some spouses, fully aware of what they had signed, were trying to use the absence of the provision of independent advice as a scheme to avoid having to honour their guarantees.

The guarantor's rights against the debtor

Under the common law, if a guarantor has to honour a guarantee, the guarantor is allowed a right of relief against the debtor—for what it is worth. If a debtor is unable to pay his debt to his creditor so that a guarantee has to be honoured, the debtor is generally in no position to repay the guarantor. But if at a later date the debtor, say, inherits some money, the guarantor may still claim against the debtor (assuming the claim has not prescribed) (*Smithy's Place Ltd v Blackadder & McMonagle* (1991)). If a guarantor has had fully to honour a guarantee, the creditor must on request assign the benefit of any security or other rights (such as diligence) he may have against the debtor in favour of the guarantor so that the guarantor can the better enforce his right of relief against the debtor (*Thow's Trustees v Young* (1910)).

The *contra proferentem* rule

If there is ambiguity in the wording of a guarantee, and if one party (usually the stronger party, the creditor) is seeking to rely on the ambiguity of the wording to favour his own interests, the wording is construed in a manner that is contrary to the interest of the person drawing up the contract of guarantee (*Aitken's Trs. v Bank of Scotland* (1944)).

Misrepresentation

Where a debtor induces a guarantor by misrepresentation to sign a guarantee, the guarantee is still valid and the guarantor merely has a right of action against the debtor, though this may be of little benefit to him (*Young v Clydesdale Bank* (1889)). A creditor's failure to reveal information about the debtor to the guarantor does not invalidate a guarantee, since it is up to the guarantor to satisfy himself that it is safe to offer a guarantee for the debtor's debts to the creditor (*Royal Bank of Scotland v Greenshields* (1914)); but if the guarantor actually asks the creditor for information about the debtor (either in writing or orally) the creditor must not misrepresent the position and if the guarantor relies on that misrepresentation, whether it is made fraudulently or innocently, he may resile from the guarantee (*Royal Bank of Scotland v Ranken* (1844)). In practice nowadays it is likely that any creditor given such a request would say that the guarantor must make his own enquiries.

Termination of the guarantee

Once the principal debt is repaid, the guarantee is discharged. But where the debt is discharged on the debtor's bankruptcy, the guarantee still continues in existence (Bankruptcy (Scotland) Act 1985, s.60) and indeed will almost certainly be called upon. The benefit of a guarantee may be assigned, unless there is some term in the guarantee forbidding this and providing that the assignation is intimated to the cautioner. During the course of the guarantee the creditor is not permitted to make the cautioner's position worse than the position he had accepted when he entered into the guarantee (*Huewind Ltd v Clydesdale Bank plc* (1995)).

The death of the debtor prevents any further liability under the guarantee, but the guarantor remains liable for whatever he may have contracted for up to that point (*Woodfield Finance Trust (Glasgow) Ltd v Morgan* (1958)). The death of the guarantor transfers the guarantor's liability to his estate unless the guarantee says otherwise. If there are several guarantors, and one of them is discharged without the others being discharged or without their consent, then all of the guarantors are discharged, unless the guarantee says otherwise (Mercantile Law Amendment (Scotland) Act 1856, s.9). Under the Prescription and Limitation (Scotland) Act 1973, s.6 a creditor loses his rights to enforce a guarantee within a period of five years after the guarantee becomes enforceable if those rights have not been acknowledged or enforced within that time.

30 *Commercial Law*

Further reading

Clark and Eden, "Cautionary Obligations," in *Stair Memorial Encyclopedia* (Law Society of Scotland/Butterworths, 1994), Vol.3.
Forte (ed.), *Scots Commercial Law* (Butterworths, 1997), Chap.6.
Gloag and Henderson, *The Law of Scotland* (11th ed., W. Green, 2001), Chap.19.
Grier, *Banking Law in Scotland* (W. Green 2001), Chap.9
Mays (ed.), *Scots Law: A Student Guide* (T&T Clark, 2000), 8–40 to 8–44.

---

5. NEGOTIABLE INSTRUMENTS

Negotiable instruments are a method, using signed documents, of transferring funds from one person to another, other than by using cash or by modern methods of electronic transfer. The law relating to bills of exchange underpins the law relating to cheques. The word "negotiable" means that a bill may be transferred from one person to another as if it were cash, so that the paper instruction of one person to pay another becomes almost as good as handing cash over in payment for goods.

The benefits of bills of exchange
Alan buys goods costing £10,000 from Ben on February 1. Unfortunately Alan cannot pay for the goods on that day, but Alan is owed £10,000 from Charles, due to be paid March 1. Alan could draw up a bill of exchange that would state that Charles was to pay Ben £10,000 on March 1. Charles would accept the bill, that is, acknowledge that he will have to pay the bill on the due date, and forward it to Ben. Ben then has an entitlement to £10,000. Furthermore, as the bill is a free-standing obligation in its own right irrespective of the underlying transaction, if Ben's goods turned out to be faulty and Alan refused to accept them, the bill of exchange would still be valid and Charles would have to honour the bill of exchange. Alan would then have to sue Ben for the faulty goods instead, but Charles could not withhold payment.

If Ben needs his money now, rather than waiting a month for it, Ben may sell or "negotiate" the bill to David. David might buy the bill for, say, £9,800, the discount of £200 reflecting Ben's need for cash now, the risk of Charles defaulting on payment, and the loss of a month's interest on £10,000. David could sell the bill to Edward. Even if Edward had defrauded David to obtain the bill, Edward could still sell the bill on to Francis, who, provided he bought the bill from Edward in good faith without notice of there being anything wrong with the bill, and provided the bill was on the face of it valid, could nevertheless ultimately receive payment from Charles.

Negotiation of a bill is not quite the same as transfer: in general, when a bill is transferred, the recipient does not necessarily get good title (*i.e.* undisputed ownership of the right to payment) to the bill that he has received, whereas with negotiation, the recipient does get good title.

The nature of a bill of exchange

A bill of exchange is essentially an instruction by one person (in the following example "Alan Armour") to a second person ("Charles Campbell") that Charles should pay a specified sum to a third person ("Ben Buchan") at a specified date. The Bills of Exchange Act 1882 ("BOE"), s.3 states as follows:

> A bill of exchange is an unconditional order in writing, addressed by one person to another, signed by the person giving it, requiring the person to whom it is addressed to pay on demand or at a fixed or determinable future time a sum certain in money to or to the order of a specified person, or to bearer.

Here is an example:

Bill of exchange for £10,000   Edinburgh, February 1, 2003
At thirty (30) days after date pay Ben Buchan or order the sum of ten thousand pounds Sterling. For value received.
To Charles Campbell   (Signed) Alan Armour
1 Perth Avenue,
Galashiels

The person who instructs the order, Alan, is known as the "drawer" of the bill. He must sign the bill or it is invalid. Signing the bill works in two ways: it serves as proof of the instruction to the person paying the bill, Charles, but it also makes the drawer, Alan, liable at a later date if the bill is dishonoured (*i.e.* not paid when it should be).

The person who receives the order or instruction to pay the bill, Charles, is known as the "drawee". The process of ordering the payment of the bill is known "as drawing a bill". When a bank pays a cheque, it is acting as a drawee by receiving its customer's order to pay the money to the customer's intended recipient.

The recipient of the money on payment, Ben, is the "payee". When the bill is first drawn, the payee's name will be stated (unless it is made payable to bearer) and the payee will expect to receive payment. If, however, Ben as payee negotiates the bill to someone else, David, Ben loses his entitlement to payment and the new holder of the bill, David, becomes the next payee.

"Bearer" means a person who is bearing the bill, *i.e.* has it in his possession. Where a bill is made out to bearer, the bill may be transferred by delivery (BOE, s.31(2)).

A "holder" is similar to a bearer in that he is a person who is "holding" the bill of exchange, or in other words who has it in his possession, but in addition he is normally entitled to payment on it. Holders are discussed in greater detail later. Bills may not be made out to holder.

The amount payable is stated to be "a sum certain in money" (BOE, s.9). This means exactly what it says, so that the figure stated must be calculable (if there is interest due) and payable in money as opposed to any other commodity.

There must be no conditions attached to the bill or it will lose its status as a bill (BOE, s.3(2)). The date of payment must be fixed or at least determinable (BOE, s.11). It is common to have bills payable in periods of 30 days, but it is possible to have a bill payable on demand, or on sight or on presentment. But a time bill, which gives a specific date, may only be paid on or after that date.

Indorsement

When a bill that is payable "or order" (as in the above example) is transferred, the practice is for the payee to sign his name on the back of the bill. The words "or order" signify that the payee may choose an alternative recipient of the payment. Signing the bill is known as indorsement and, when followed by delivery to the recipient, is an effective negotiation of the bill (BOE, s.31(3)). In turn the recipient (the "indorsee") might wish to transfer the bill to someone specific, in which case he too would indorse his name and add the words "Pay AB" and hand the bill to AB, the new indorsee. This is known as special indorsement (BOE, s.34(2)) and limits the transferability of the bill to AB alone, though AB could negotiate it further if he wished to do so. It is possible to restrict the transfer by ascribing the indorser's name and adding "Pay AB only", thus making it a restrictive indorsement (BOE, s.35(2)). The bill then ceases to be negotiable to anyone other than AB (BOE, s.35(2)). If the bill is made payable to bearer, there is no need for signatures; all that is required is delivery (BOE, s.31(2)). An order bill ought to be indorsed to show who the intended indorsee is, but if none is specified, the bill then becomes "blank indorsed" and is treated as a bearer bill (BOE, s.34(1)). If a blank indorsed bill is stolen, the thief may easily obtain payment—which is why bearer bills are rare. The recipient of a blank indorsed bill can protect himself by signing his name where it could have been inserted by the indorser, thus converting the blank indorsement into a special indorsement (BOE, s.34(4)).

A person who indorses a bill has to accept the fact that by indorsing the bill he may have to compensate the indorsee (or subsequent indorser) should the bill not be paid (BOE, s.55(2)(a)). He may not subsequently assert that he is not liable on the bill because the drawer's signature or any previous indorsers' signatures were forged or irregular (BOE, s.55(2)(b)) or that he did not have good title to the bill anyway (BOE, s.55(2)(c)).

Acceptance by the drawee of the bill

For a bill of exchange to be effective on a practical basis, the drawee must know that he has to pay the bill to the payee. He does this by accepting the bill when it is first sent to him by the drawer (BOE, s.17). He formally writes on the bill the word "accepted" along with his name. This is not necessary for cheques or promissory notes. The drawee's acceptance of the bill results in his redesignation as an "acceptor", and he will normally then forward the bill to the payee. Without acceptance, the bill may be less valuable because acceptance is a formal acknowledgment of the drawee's awareness of his duty to pay. It is possible to give a qualified acceptance (BOE, s.19(2)), though a wise payee will refuse it as he is entitled to do (BOE, s.44(1)), since the condition imposed under the qualification might be something beyond his immediate control.

A drawee may refuse to accept the bill. This is known as dishonour by non-acceptance and it makes the drawer who signed the bill liable instead (BOE, s.43(2)). This is because it is possible that the drawer has no dealings with the drawee and is effectively trying to defraud the drawee, or mislead the payee into believing that the drawee will pay the payee; alternatively the drawee does not have the funds to honour the bill. If the drawer has transferred the unaccepted bill to subsequent indorsers, each of them is potentially liable to the ultimate holder of the bill as well (BOE, s.43(2)), though the holder must first notify the dishonour to the drawer and to each indorser (BOE, s.48) and those who are not notified will not be liable (BOE, s.48).

Assuming the bill is accepted, in due course the bill will have to be re-presented to the acceptor by the payee or the ultimate holder for payment when the time for payment comes. However, if the acceptor then refuses to pay the bill further steps will be required. These will be discussed shortly.

Where the drawee is a fictitious person or someone without contractual capacity, the drawer will be trying to negotiate a bill that has no underlying obligation on a drawee to pay. In this case the drawer will become liable for it (BOE, s.5(2)).

THE HOLDER IN DUE COURSE

The holder

As stated above, the first person due to receive payment under a bill is the payee. Where the payee transfers the bill to someone else, either by indorsement and delivery, or by delivery if the payee is a bearer, the person holding the bill is known as the holder. Even if a fraudster who obtained a bill by fraud is a holder, though he has a voidable title to the bill (BOE, s.30(2)). If the bill is stolen, the bill still remains the property of the former owner, though in practice it becomes very difficult to prevent the holder either selling the bill on to another holder or presenting it to the acceptor for payment. A holder is entitled to sue for payment, but under BOE, s.30(2), if there is a defect in the title, he may be unable to assert his claim. So if a thief holding a bill tries to obtain payment of a bill, but the victim told the acceptor first that the bill had been stolen, the acceptor would not need to pay the bill and the thief could not sue the drawer or any subsequent indorsee for payment either. A holder's claim is strengthened if he is (a) a holder for value, and (b) also a holder in due course.

Holder for value

A holder for value is a person who has either paid to acquire a bill of exchange himself, or a prior holder has paid for it (BOE, s.27(1), (2)). This provision is necessary because of the English law of consideration.

Holder in due course

A holder in due course is in the happy position, as indicated earlier, of being well protected and well able to obtain payment under the bill, provided the following conditions are satisfied under BOE, s.29(1):

(a) the bill must be complete and regular on the face of it, so that as far as can be seen it contains all the essential requirements of a properly drawn up bill;
(b) the bill is not overdue;
(c) the holder is unaware of any previous dishonour of the bill, either by non-acceptance or non-payment;
(d) the holder must have acquired the bill in good faith;
(e) the holder must have been unaware of any defect in title in the previous holder who negotiated the bill to him.

If all these criteria are satisfied, the holder becomes a holder in due course and may obtain a better title to the bill than the person who negotiated the bill to him, even if somewhere in the course of the bill's progress it has been obtained fraudulently. If the bill is dishonoured by the acceptor, the holder in due course may claim against the drawer and indorsers (BOE, s.43(2)).

Presentment for payment

The holder will normally present the bill for payment to the acceptor, who will pay the bill (BOE, s.54). If the payment is not made, it is said to be "dishonoured", thus making the drawer and/or indorsers liable instead (BOE, s.47). The holder must give notice of dishonour to the drawer and each indorser (BOE, s.48) who can then be sued for non-payment if necessary (BOE, s.57). Inland bills may and foreign bills must be "protested", which is a formal procedure before a notary public and which is public notice of the failure of the acceptor to pay (BOE, s.51).

The effect of forgery

Forgery of a signature renders the person whose signature has been forged free from liability (BOE, s.24). A holder in due course, who normally is well protected from other misadventures involving bills, loses his protection where there has been a forgery. However, he is protected to some extent, because an acceptor may not refuse to pay a bill on the grounds that the drawer's signature is a forgery (BOE, s.54(2)). He will also be protected where the payee is non-existent or fictitious, since such a bill is treated as a bearer bill and can be presented for payment (BOE, s.7(3)).

The position of cheques will be dealt with later in this Chapter in the relevant section.

Alteration

Where a bill is materially altered, without the consent of all those party to it, it becomes voidable. The person who altered it without authority will remain liable on it, along with any subsequent indorsers (BOE, s.64(1)). A holder in due course who is unaware of the alteration because it is not easily noticeable on the face of it will, however, be able to claim on the bill (BOE, s.64(1)). Where the alteration is immaterial the bill remains valid. Immaterial alterations are such acts as crossing a cheque (BOE, s.77) or inserting a date (BOE, s.12).

Discharge of bills

Bills are discharged when they are paid by the acceptor (BOE, s.59). Where the holder and the acceptor are the same person, as may occasionally happen in commercial matters, the bill is also discharged. If the drawer is found liable on the bill, payment of the bill does not discharge it, since the drawer may have a right of relief against some other person (BOE, s.59(2)). A bill may be renounced by the holder, who may choose not to enforce payment, but if so, this must be clearly and unconditionally expressed in writing (BOE, s.62). A holder may also cancel a bill under BOE, s.63.

Prescription

Bills of exchange, cheque and promissory notes prescribe after five years, in accordance with the Prescription and Limitation (Scotland) Act 1973, s.6(1), Sch.1, para.1(e).

CHEQUES

A cheque is a bill of exchange, payable on demand, drawn on a banker (BOE, s.73). The drawer is the person writing the cheque, the drawee is the bank and the payee is the person to whom the money will be paid. Acceptance does not arise in the context of cheques. Cheques are paid on demand, though it is possible to have a post-dated cheque. Crossing a cheque means that the funds to be paid out on the cheque may only be paid to the payee's bank account, and payee cannot obtain cash from the drawer's bank account (BOE, s.79(2)). A special crossing is one where the crossing, by two parallel lines, contains the name of the bank to which payment must be made. This is rare in domestic banking. More common is a general crossing, which consists of two parallel lines and the words "A/C Payee", "Account Payee" or "Account Payee only" and in theory this requires payment to the payee's bank account only (BOE, s.80) and makes the cheque untransferable (BOE, s.81A(1)). If a bank does pay in cash a cheque with such a crossing on it to someone who has, say, stolen the cheque, the bank will have to reimburse the account holder and the person from whom the cheque was stolen (BOE, s.79(2)). A cheque that is crossed "not negotiable" may be transferred, but the transferee obtains no better title than the transferor (BOE, s.81), and could therefore lose the normal protection of being a holder in due course.

Protection for banks

If a bank in good faith and without negligence pays a cheque into a bank account in accordance with its crossing, the bank is treated as if it had paid the cheque to the true owner of the cheque, which means that even if the cheque has been stolen the drawer's account may still be debited (BOE, s.80) even if the cheque was not transferable in terms of BOE, s.81A. Equally, where a bank in good faith and without negligence receives a cheque for a customer and pays it into his account, and thereafter takes from the customer's account any sums due to the bank, if it transpires that the customer did not have title to the cheque, the bank will not be liable to the true owner of the cheque merely because it received payment via its customer (Cheques Act 1957, s.4(1)). This is true even if the cheque is not transferable (Cheques Act, 1957 s.4(2)).

In practice what normally happens with a stolen cheque is that the victim of the theft will tell the drawer to stop the cheque in order to prevent payment.

Indorsement of cheques

Most cheques nowadays are pre-printed with crossings already on them, thus making it difficult to indorse cheques. Much of the old law about indorsement of cheques is therefore in practice obsolete.

Where a holder in due course presents an indorsed and uncrossed cheque for payment, if the banker pays out cash to the holder in good faith and in the ordinary course of business, the holder may receive payment and the drawer's account will be debited (BOE, s.60). This is true even if the payee's indorsement has been forged, since the bank cannot be expected to check every indorsement for forgery (Cheques Act 1957, s.1).

Expiry of cheques

As a matter of banking practice and by convention, cheques are said to become "stale" after six months and will need to be re-issued.

PROMISSORY NOTES

The law relating to promissory notes may be found at BOE, ss. 83–89. A promissory note is an unconditional undertaking by one person to another, in writing, that on a fixed or determinable time he will pay a sum certain money to another person (the payee), or to someone else as instructed by the payee. Promissory notes can be negotiated in the same manner as bills of exchange, and nearly all of BOE applies to promissory notes as it does to bills of exchange, save that the provisions relating to presentment for acceptance and presentment for payment do not apply. Promissory notes may be protested and summary diligence may proceed as with bills of exchange.

Further reading

Elliot, *Byles on Bills of Exchange and Cheques* (27th ed., Sweet & Maxwell, 2001).
Chalmers and Guest, *Bills of Exchange* (15th ed., Sweet & Maxwell, 1998).
Forte (ed.), *Scots Commercial Law* (Butterworths, 1997), Chap.5.
Gloag and Henderson, *The Law of Scotland* (11th ed., W. Green, 2001), Chap.22.
Grier, *Banking Law in Scotland* (W.Green, 2001), Chap.8

6. INSURANCE

A contract of insurance arises where one person ("the insurer") in consideration of a payment, known as a premium, takes on the financial or other consequences (known as risk) which amount to an uncertain event that may befall another person ("the insured") or his assets at or before a future date, certain or uncertain, whereby the insurer is required to pay money to or make good any loss to the insured on the occasion of the uncertain event.

The law applicable to insurance

Insurance is mostly governed by the common law, though the Marine Insurance Act 1906 restated and codified much of the common law in a statutory form. It is often referred to because it contains much of the best practice that insurance policies should follow. Insurance contracts are carefully worded and the insurer's liability often depends on whether the situation giving rise to a claim falls within the ambit of the words that have been chosen. Commercial insurance is not covered by the Unfair Contract Terms Act 1977, but consumer insurance is covered by the

Unfair Terms in Consumer Contracts Regulations 1999, Also in the context of consumer insurance, most insurers adhere to the insurance industry's voluntary codes, the Statement of General Insurance Practice and the Statement of Long-Term Insurance Practice. In commercial contracts of insurance, insurers and policy holders depend on the common law and where appropriate the Marine Insurance Act 1906. Where an insurance policy combines an investment element, the Financial Services Act 1986 and Financial Services and Markets Act 2000 apply in respect of the investment element.

The insurance industry generally is regulated by the Insurance Companies Act 1982. The Act ensures that insurance companies maintain minimum solvency levels and are properly managed. Insurance brokers are regulated by, amongst other legislation, the Insurance Brokers (Registration) Act 1977, the Financial Services Act 1986 and the Financial Services and Markets Act 2000. The Financial Services Authority serves as the regulatory agency empowered to monitor the insurance industry in the United Kingdom.

Complaints about the business and practices of insurance companies may be dealt with by the Financial Ombudsman Service. The Ombudsman is an independent agency with the power to investigate and settle disputes, particularly disputes between consumers and insurers.

Life assurance policies may be written in trust for the family of the insured (Married Women's Policies of Assurance (Scotland) Act 1880).

The terms of the insurance contract

In order to effect an insurance contract, the person who wants to have the benefit of the insurance policy, the proposer, completes a proposal form issued by the insurance company (the insurer as above). The proposal forms, which are commonly standardised, outline the terms on which insurance companies do business. The proposer's completion of the proposal form is an offer to the insurance company, which it can accept or reject depending on the information given. Typically the insurance company will conditionally accept the offer, subject to payment of the first premium and clarification of any outstanding points. Once the proposer's proposal is accepted, and an insurance policy issued by the insurance company, the proposer becomes known as the "policyholder". The period of insurance usually starts from acceptance of payment of the first premium, though exceptionally it may start beforehand if agreed between the parties. There is no liability if there is no contract (in *Canning v Farquhar* (1886), Canning fell off a cliff; at the time his first premium had been tendered but not accepted, and without acceptance of the premium there was no contract and no liability for the insurers).

***Uberrimae fidei* and the duty of disclosure**

The principle on which insurance proposals operate is that of *uberrimae fidei*, this meaning "the utmost good faith". So if a proposal form asks a question, it must be answered truthfully and fully and all material facts must be disclosed. In *The Spathari* (1925), the proposer deliberately concealed the underlying Greek ownership of a ship, thus breaching his duty to provide all information with and in the utmost good faith. "Material" is defined in the Marine Insurance Act 1906, s.12(2): "Every circumstance is material which would influence the judgment of a prudent insurer in fixing the premium or determining whether he will take the risk."

The duty of utmost good faith means that it is not enough for the proposer to rely on the phrase "to the best of my knowledge and belief" where a little research or common sense might disclose information which would be material to the insurer (in *McPhee v Royal Insurance Co. Ltd* (1979), the proposer provided second-hand and inaccurate measurements of a boat).

Further material matters that need to be disclosed often include previous convictions (unless they are deemed to be spent under the Rehabilitation of Offenders Act 1974), the occupation of the insured, any dangerous hobbies of the insured, previous losses which were the subject of a claim and the state of the insured's health.

Matters which generally are not considered material are: such matters as diminish the insurer's risk; facts that are deemed to be common knowledge; facts about the law; facts which the insurance company checks for itself; and facts that would not be relevant to a claim. Sometimes there is doubt as to whether or not something is material, and it would appear that in England the test of materiality is that of the reasonable insurer, but in Scotland, in the context of life assurance only, the test is that of the reasonable insured (*Life Association of Scotland v Foster* (1873), affirmed in *Hooper v Royal London General Insurance Co. Ltd* (1993)). As regards non-life assurance, the test would appear to be that of the reasonable insurer (*Hooper*).

Continuing duty of disclosure
Although in general there is no continuing duty of disclosure, if the insurance contract states that a material change in circumstances must be disclosed to the insurer, that must indeed be done or the policy will fall. In any case, each time the policy renewal notice appears with a request for a new payment of the premium, there is a new contract formed, albeit on the same basis as before, so that the duty to disclose arises on each occasion of the renewal of the policy.

It is a disputed question whether disclosure to an agent amounts to disclosure to the insurance company. It would appear that where the proposer had disclosed information to an agent in good faith and without intention to defraud, the insurance company still had to honour the policy despite the fact that the agent, unbeknownst to the proposer, had misrepresented the true position, as in *Bawden v London, Edinburgh and Glasgow Assurance Co.* (1892). This can be contrasted with another case, *Newsholme Bros v Road Transport and General Insurance Co. Ltd* (1929), where the agent inserted inaccurate information on the proposal form. In this case the proposer knew of the inaccuracy but signed it anyway. The agent was held in this case to have acted for the insured person and not for the insurance company, and the insurance company was able to avoid the contract for misrepresentation.

Warranties

A warranty is: (a) a form of promise by the insured that a certain act will be done, or continue to be done, or as the case may be, will not be done, or that some condition will be fulfilled; or (b) a confirmation that a particular state of affairs does or does not exist. Warranties about the past do not carry forward to the future unless the wording says otherwise. Warranties do not need to be material: they need to be defined as warranties, and if the insured does not carry out the undertaking in the warranty, or if the state of affairs referred to in a warranty about the past did not take place in the manner stated, the insurer incurs no further liability with effect from the date of the breach of the warranty (Marine Insurance Act 1906, s.33(3)).

The effect of a warranty may be seen in *Dawsons Ltd v Bonnin* (1922), where a proposer warranted on a proposal form that a lorry was kept in a stone building in central Glasgow. The lorry was later burnt in a fire in a wooden garage elsewhere in Glasgow, and it was held that the breach of the warranty avoided the contract. It does not matter how material the warranty may be: what is significant is whether or not the warranty has been carried out, has been or is being observed, or is or was correct. So if a clause is described as a warranty, it must be observed to the letter.

The *contra proferentem* rule and the wording of contracts generally

The rule in insurance contracts is that the meaning of the words used in such contracts is their normal everyday meaning, unless there is clear indication that some other technical meaning is used instead. If there is ambiguity in the contract, and the insurance company is trying to rely on the ambiguity of the wording of the contract to avoid liability, the construction of the wording will be interpreted contrary to the interest of the insurance company that drew up the contract. As a matter of practice, insurance contracts have gradually become easier to understand, partly through the influence of such bodies as the Plain English Campaign, partly through the *contra proferentem* rule, and partly because of the inadequate wording of earlier contracts which resulted in liability for the insurance company. In *Harris v Poland* (1941), an elderly lady had taken out insurance for "loss" of her jewels "by fire". Before going on holiday, she carefully hid her jewels in some old newspaper and under some unlit coal in her grate. On her return she felt cold and absentmindedly lit the fire, thus damaging her jewels. She claimed for the loss by fire of her jewels and was duly successful. Had the policy said "self-induced loss" the insurer would not have been liable.

But where the wording is clear, and the insured fails to do what he is supposed to do, such as intimate a claim in time, or take reasonable precautions, there is no liability.

Insurable interest
Since the passing of the Life Assurance Act 1774, the insured must have an insurable interest in the thing or person insured, and the interest must be a genuine family, business or other close connection. There must be a genuine insurable interest held by the insured in insured property: in *MacAura v Northern Assurance Property Ltd* (1925), MacAura insured in his own name growing timber which was actually owned by a limited company. When it burnt down, he claimed the insurance proceeds in his own name, but was refused because the timber was owned by the company and he personally had no insurable interest in the growing timber.

Causation
The peril that is insured against must be the proximate cause of the loss giving rise to the claim. In *Leyland Shipping Co. Ltd v Norwich Union Fire Insurance Society* (1918), a marine policy excluded liability relating to damage from enemy action. An insured ship was torpedoed by a German submarine and was towed to Le Havre. It was not allowed to berth there lest it sank and blocked the harbour. It was towed to a spot outside the harbour where it later grounded and sank. The insurers avoided liability on the grounds that the proximate cause was the torpedoing by the enemy, not the grounding.

Miscellaneous terms in insurance policies
In an indemnity policy the policy holder may not make a profit on the claim: he should recover his loss and no more. But it is possible to contract that in the event of a specified event happening, the value of which may be hard to estimate in advance, an agreed sum will be paid out for a total loss, even if in fact this may be more or less than the actual value of the loss. This is known as an *agreed value policy*.

A *reinstatement value policy* is one where the policy pays out enough to reinstate the property to the condition it was in before the insured event happened. Some property insurance policies sold in conjunction with standard securities insist that the proceeds of the policy must be used to restore the property.

A *"new for old"* policy does not aim merely to give the value of the asset as at the date of its destruction, but the value of a new asset of the same type. The premiums are correspondingly higher than for an ordinary replacement policy.

An *excess clause* requires the policy holder to pay, say, the first £100 of a claim. This discourages frivolous claims and may enable the policy holder better to retain a no-claims bonus, whereby the cost of the premiums diminish the longer the holder goes without having a claim.

Over-insurance is where an insured is paying premiums for a higher rate of insurance than the insured property is worth, perhaps because the property has depreciated. In the event of loss, it is the actual extent of the loss that will be paid, and the insured will have effectively been wasting his money by over-insuring. *Under-insurance* is where an asset is insured for less than its true worth, often because the cost of the premiums is too high for the policy holder. When a claim takes place, the insurer only pays out to the value of the sum insured, which may be much less than the value of the asset. Average is the term for the calculation of the extent of the insurer's liability in the event of under-insurance. If an asset is valued at £20,000 but is insured for £16,000, and £8,000 worth of damage occurs, the insurance company pays a proportion of the loss: in this case it would pay sixteen-twentieths of £8,000, being £6,400. The balance must be found by the owner.

Contribution occurs where there is more than one insurer for the same asset. Unless the terms of the insurance policies are identical this can result in long and complicated battles over liability.

Subrogation arises where an insured is potentially able to claim both from an insurer and from the person who caused him damage, as in a car accident. Where an insurer pays an insured following an accident, the insurer can then step into the shoes, as it were, of the insured to recoup its loss from the other driver (or his insurance company).

Assignation of policies is a normal procedure, particularly for life policies, whereby the benefit to the proceeds of a life policy is transferred to someone else. Assignation must be accompanied in Scotland by intimation to the insurance company (Transmission of Moveable Property (Scotland) Act 1862).

Third-party insurance arises mostly in the context of vehicle insurance where it is compulsory (Road Traffic Act 1972, s.143). Third-party insurance covers damage to other vehicles or people, whereas first-party insurance merely covers damage to yourself or your vehicle.

Endowment life assurance policies are a combination of insurance and investment: the premiums that the policy holder pays are invested in such a manner that not only will the policy pay out a fixed sum on death within the predetermined period (the insurance element), but will also pay out a sum at the end of the period which is the proceeds of the invested sums and the reinvested returns on the invested premiums. In this way the assurance policy provides both protection for the insured and a savings vehicle.

There are certain occasions where insurance is compulsory: for example employers (other than the Government and local authorities) must be insured under the Employers' Liability (Compulsory Insurance) Act 1969, and solicitors have to be signed up to the Master Policy, organised by the Law Society of Scotland.

Some drivers, illegally, drive when they are not insured. If they cause an accident, the Motor Insurance Bureau, a body set up by the main insurance companies, acts as their insurance company and may pay out any claims made by victims of accidents involving uninsured drivers.

Further reading

Birds, *Modern Insurance Law* (5th ed., Sweet & Maxwell, 2001).
Forte (ed.), *Scots Commercial Law* (Butterworths, 1997), Chap.4.
Gloag and Henderson, *The Law of Scotland* (11th ed., W. Green, 2001), Chap.23.
Mays, *Scots Law, A Student Guide* (T&T Clark, 2001), 8–112 to 8–126.
Leigh-Jones *MacGillivray on Insurance Law* (10th ed., Sweet & Maxwell, 2003).

7. AGENCY

An agent is a person who acts on behalf of a principal, bringing him into a legal relationship with a third party, but without himself necessarily being involved in that relationship. In effect there are two contracts in agency, one between the agent and the principal, and one between the principal and the third party. Common types of agent are estate agents, brokers of various kinds (stock, mortgages, insurance, ships, etc.), solicitors, publishers' agents, etc. Normally, but not exclusively, the agent is rewarded by means of a commission or fee from the principal.

An agent who by convention is given a broad area of authority to act on behalf of the principal (such as a solicitor) is known as a "general" agent, while one who is given specific instructions for a specific purpose only is known as a "special" agent (such as a travel agent). Where a special agent steps beyond the remit given to him by his principal, the principal will not in general be liable to those who deal with the special agent in areas beyond his remit.

CONSTITUTION OF AGENCY

There are different ways in which an agency may be set up, but the main ways are:

(a) agency by express appointment;
(b) agency by implied appointment;
(c) agency by ratification;
(d) agency by necessity;
(e) agency by holding out;
(f) *del credere* agency.

The parties to a contract of agency must have legal capacity and must exist. Where the principal does not exist, but legal obligations arise, as in a contract made by a director of an as yet unformed company, the purported agent (in this case the purported director) will himself be liable for the obligations arising out of the contract (*Phonogram Ltd v Lane* (1982)), unless the contract says otherwise (see the Companies Act 1985, s.36C).

Agency need not be constituted in writing, though commercial agents are entitled to obtain from their principals, and principals from their agents, a statement of the terms on which they will do business with each other (Commercial Agents (Council Directive) Regulations 1993, reg.13). These regulations prescribe certain standard rules applicable to contracts of agency giving agents normal commercial rights and to some extent protecting them from unscrupulous principals. Although the parties are given some freedom to derogate from the requirements of the Regulations, most of the Regulations are unalterable and will override the common law of agency (*Roy v M R Pearlman* 1999). The main provisions of the Regulations allow commercial agents the right to remuneration at a reasonable rate, and the right to fair notice of termination with compensation for premature termination. In return the agent has to accept duties of confidentiality and sensible restraint of trade provisions, and act dutifully and in good faith for the principal who in turn must act dutifully and in good faith towards the agent, having suitably provided him with the necessary information to carry out his tasks.

Agency by express appointment

The deliberate appointment of an agent by a principal, and the grant of authority to act on the principal's behalf, whether constituted by written contract or not, is known as agency by express appointment.

Agency by implication

An agency may arise through the actings of the parties, even though there has been no express appointment (see *Barnetson v Petersen Brothers* (1902), where a shipbroker was held to have been employed to act as agent for the shipowners by virtue of his actions on their behalf and to which they had not objected). Agency may also be implied by operation of law: for example, a partner acts as agent for his partnership (Partnership Act 1890, s.5).

Agency by ratification

The agency agreement need not pre-date the agent's actions: an agent might carry out an act for a principal who was unaware that the agent had acted for him, but on the principal's awareness of the act, the principal may ratify (*i.e.* retrospectively authorise) the act, either by a positive action or by his conduct. Four conditions, other than the legality of the contract, are required for ratification:

(a) the agent must act as agent, and must have intimated to the third party that he was acting as agent, and not on his own account (*Keighley Maxted & Co. v Durant* (1901));

(b) the principal must exist (*Boston Deep Sea Fishing v Farnham* (1957));

(c) the principal must have the requisite legal capacity, so that a contract struck at by the Age of Legal Capacity (Scotland) Act 1991 would not be binding on a child.

(d) the principal must be informed of all the acts that the agent has carried out on his behalf (*Fitzmaurice v Bayley*).

It has been argued that timeous ratification is also a condition of ratification, but there are contrary decisions on this issue both in Scotland and in England and the position remains unclear.

Agency of necessity

An agency of necessity arises where an agent carries out vital acts for a principal without receiving instructions. This is also known as *negotiorum gestio*. With the advent of satellite communication it is now rare for agencies of necessity to arise except in extreme climatic conditions or in a state of war. It occasionally arises where people are too ill to issue instructions, so that others are forced to act on their behalf (see *Fernie v Robertson* (1871), where a senile person's estate was liable for house repair bills contracted on her behalf by an agent of necessity).

Agency by holding out

This arises either when a principal takes no steps to contradict the impression that an individual is his agent or positively encourages that impression. If a third party relies on that impression, it would be unfair of the principal to reverse that impression, particularly if in the meantime the third party has acted to his detriment (see *Freeman & Lockyer v Buckhurst Park Properties (Mangal) Ltd* (1964), where a company took no steps to reverse the impression that one of its directors was authorised to act on its behalf). Exceptionally, where the agent gives the impression that the principal will approve the agent's actions, the principal may be liable for not contradicting that impression at an early stage (*First Energy (UK) Ltd v Hungarian International Bank* (1993)).

Del credere agency

A *del credere* agency is one where the agent guarantees payment or performance by the third party. The agent effectively bears the risk of the transaction. Such agencies are rare nowadays.

THE LIABILITY OF THE PRINCIPAL FOR THE AGENT'S ACTINGS

Normally an agent will act within the limits of the authority imposed on him by his principal and the principal will therefore be liable for the agent's actings, as he also will be if he ratifies the agent's actings. However, occasionally an agent will overstep those limits, sometimes in the perceived best interests of the principal, or sometimes fraudulently. In *Panorama Developments (Guildford) Ltd v Fidelis Furnishings Fabric Ltd* (1971), a company secretary hired cars from a car hire company ostensibly as part of his duties. His employers were held liable for his car-hire bills, even though he had in fact used the cars on private business, on the grounds that the car-hire company could reasonably have assumed that he was using the cars on company business.

Where an agent: (a) exceeds his authority; but (b) acts in such a way that a third party has no reason to suspect that the agent is exceeding his authority; and (c) the principal has not intimated the agent's lack of authority to the third party, the principal may be liable for the agent's unauthorised act. In *Watteau v Fenwick* (1893), a public house manager bought cigars from a salesman despite express instructions from the manager's employers not to do so. The employers were still liable for the cigars because the salesman was unaware that the manager did not have the requisite authority. This case has been much criticised, but it is authority for the proposition that the principal may not rely on a limitation of authority that is not communicated to a third party.

Apparent or ostensible authority
This arises where a principal suffers a state of affairs to exist or a course of dealing to be perpetuated which gives the outside world the impression that the agent has the authority to act as he has done, unless it would be very unlikely that the principal would approve a particular unauthorised act (see *International Sponge Importers Ltd v Watt & Sons* (1911), where a salesman had specifically been permitted by his principal to receive payments in his own name, thus making the principal liable and the contrasting case of *British Bata Shoe Co. Ltd v Double M Shah Ltd* (1980), where the employer had no knowledge of, and would not have approved of the actions of an employee in persuading customers to pay the employee personally rather than the employer). It also arises where an agent performs actions which are appropriate for his position (as in *Panorama v Fidelis* and *Watteau v Fenwick* above).

When a partner leaves a firm his former partners should strictly speaking announce his departure so that the firm can no longer be liable for his actions (Partnership Act 1890, s.36).

Duties of a principal to his agent
A principal is required act in good faith towards his agent and to remunerate him properly and, in the absence of any express agreement, at

a reasonable rate for the work involved (Commercial Agents (Council Directives) Regulations 1993). The contract of agency should clearly specify the conditions under which remuneration will be payable (see *Menzies, Bruce-Law and Thomson v McLennan* (1895), where commission was to be payable to agents on sale of a brewery: the sale took place, but the price was not paid; the agents were nonetheless entitled to their commission).

If an agency is to be a sole agency it should say so (*Lothian v Jenolite Ltd* (1969)). If an agent is not paid when he should be, or his expenses are not refunded, he has a right of lien over any asset of the principal's which he may have in his hands (*Glendinning v Hope & Co.* (1912)).

Non-disclosure by the agent of the principal

Where an agent sets up a contract between his named and disclosed principal and a third party, the agent is not party to the contract and is not liable on it (Bell, *Commentaries,* I, 540), unless the parties contract otherwise, as for example in a *del credere* agency. However, where the principal is undisclosed but the agent acts under the principal's express authority, the agent will be liable if he refuses to reveal the principal. This is because without this rule the third party would have no remedy against anyone (*Gibb v Cunningham & Robertson* (1925)). Where the agent is acting as an apparent principal, though in reality for an undisclosed principal, the agent and the principal are both liable unless the third party discovers who the real principal is, in which case he is entitled to elect to sue either the agent or the principal (Bell, *Commentaries,* I, 540). If it would not have been in practice difficult to establish who the principal is, the agent would not be liable (*Armour v T L Duff & Co.* (1912)).

Duties and liabilities of the agent

The agent is required to adhere to the terms of the contract between him and the principal. If he fails to carry out instructions he will be liable. In *Gilmour v Clark* (1853), the agent placed cargo in the wrong ship which then sank. The agent was held liable for the principal's loss. If the agent fails to exercise proper skill and care he will be liable. In *Luxmore-May v Messenger May Baverstock* (1990), an auctioneer severely undervalued what turned out to be a masterpiece and was held liable to the original owner for the difference between the valuation and the true value. The agent should not disclose confidential information to others (*Liverpool Victoria Friendly Society v Houston*).

In general an agent is only liable to the person with whom he is in a contractual relationship. In *Caparo Industries plc v Dickman* (1990), investing shareholders relied on an inaccurate audit, as a result of which they lost a substantial sum of money attempting a takeover. It was held that the auditors were liable to the company as a whole, not to potential individual investors.

Fiduciary duty

The principal duty of an agent to his principal is known as his fiduciary duty. This is the duty to act in good faith in the best interests of the principal, without letting any conflict of interest arise except insofar as it is permitted by the principal.

In *Boston Deep Sea Fishing Co. Ltd v Ansell* (1888), Ansell, a director of the plaintiff company, failed to reveal to the plaintiffs that he had been given a secret commission for placing certain business with a firm of shipwrights. He was required to repay it to his company.

In *McPherson's Trustees v Watt* (1877), Watt, a lawyer in Aberdeen, had been asked to deal with McPherson's estate. Watt arranged for the transfer of some of McPherson's property to Watt's brother and ultimately to himself, thus allowing a conflict of duty and interest to arise. The property transfers were accordingly reduced.

In conflict of interest cases, the only cure, apart from not letting it arise, is for the agent fully to disclose his interest and seek the consent of the principal for his course of action.

Duty not to delegate without permission

A further part of the fiduciary duty is that an agent is not permitted to delegate his tasks without the permission of the principal. This derives from the Roman law rule *Delegatus non potest delegare*. There are derogations from this in practice, such as when a solicitor delegates the conveyancing of a property to an assistant, though the solicitor will nonetheless be responsible for the assistant's work.

Duty to account

An agent is under a duty to account to his principal for all his transactions on behalf of the principal (*Simpson v Duncan* (1849)). All matters pertaining to the principal must be disclosed to him.

Breach of warranty

In *Anderson v Croall & Sons Ltd* (1903), a firm of auctioneers sold, by mistake, a horse which they had no authority to sell. The purchaser, knowing that he had a bargain, demanded that he either be given the horse (which the true owner would not release) or damages, rather than merely getting his money back. It was held that the auctioneers had breached their warranty of authority to sell, for which Anderson was entitled to damages.

TERMINATION OF AGENCY

Agency terminates by various means, including: (a) an express provision in the contract of agency; (b) the death or insanity of either the principal or agent; (c) the bankruptcy or liquidation of the principal.

If a principal wishes to ensure that he cannot possibly be liable for the actings of his agent, in an ideal world he intimates to all his customers that the agent is no longer his agent. In a large commercial organisation this is clearly impossible, and making public announcements about the termination of agencies may give customers the wrong impression. A further alternative, still often used in partnerships, is to publish a notice in the Edinburgh Gazette intimating that a former partner is no longer a partner of the firm.

Further reading

Forte (ed.), *Scots Commercial Law* (Butterworths, 1997), Chap.8.
Gloag and Henderson, *The Law of Scotland* (11th ed., W. Green, 2001), Chap.21.
Mays, *Scots Law, A Student Guide* (T&T Clark, 2001), Chap.6.
McEwan, "Agency" in *Stair Memorial Encyclopedia* (Law Society of Scotland/Butterworths, 1987), Vol.1.
O'Donnell, *Agency LawBasics* (W. Green, 1998).

8. PARTNERSHIP

Partnership is defined in the Partnership Act 1890, s.1 as "the relation which subsists between persons carrying on a business in common with a view of profit". "Persons" covers all legal personae, (excluding those persons who are *incapax*), including corporations, so that it is possible for two limited companies to join together in a partnership (sometimes known as a joint venture), or for a limited company and an individual together to be a partnership. The word "firm" in the Partnership Act 1890 ("PA") means a partnership, and the name under which the partnership practises is known as the firm name. The choice of firm name must not be contrary to the provisions of the Business Names Act 1985. A list of a firm's partners' names must be available at its place of business.

The persons involved in a partnership must be carrying on a business, so that a mere association for social purposes, such as, say, a bowling club or a dramatic society, does not qualify as a partnership. In *Khan v Miah* (1998) it was established that people proposing to set up an Indian restaurant together had not reached the stage of "carrying on a business" at the time they fell out with each other, and therefore no partnership was in existence.

The business must be in common. This means that where one person performs one activity, and another a different and unconnected activity, there would be no partnership.

Finally the partners must be operating with "a view of profit". This does not say that the partnership must make a profit; it must merely intend to do so.

The separate legal personality of a partnership
In Scotland a firm has a separate legal personality in its own right (PA, s.4(2)). In practice this makes little difference to the liability of the partners. A partnership may not own heritage in its own right, but has to have trustees to act for it (PA, s.20(2)), these being the partners.

The law of partnership is derived from the old common law, and the PA codified and standardised what had generally been understood to be the law relating to partnerships. The PA established a number of standard and widely accepted rules that apply to all partnerships, while leaving it open to individual partnerships to have other terms if they wish to do so— as most of them do. Many partnerships are not formally set up by means of a partnership agreement, and in these cases, PA gives guidelines to ascertain whether there is a partnership at all, to clarify what happens on the termination of the partnership, and how to divide the profits and losses between the partners. In addition it lays down rules for the relation of partners to each other and to outsiders. PA is also useful where there is no partnership agreement (*Starrett v Pia* (1968)) or the partnership agreement is silent on any particular point. In *Popat v Shonchhatra* (1997) the partners had failed to clarify in their partnership what should happen to post-dissolution profits. The application of PA, s.42 resolved the issue for them.

The advantages and disadvantages of partnership
There are certain advantages and disadvantages to partnership, which should be contrasted with the advantages and disadvantages of corporations and limited companies in particular (referred to in the next Chapter). The benefits of being a partner in a partnership are:

(a) colleagues with whom to share losses as well as profits;
(b) the ease and informality of setting up a partnership;
(c) rights of management in the partnership;
(d) privacy in respect of the partnership's accounts;
(e) the presence of colleagues to help share the burden of running the business;

all subject to any agreement between the partners otherwise. In practice the main benefit is the absence of any requirement to publish accounts, thereby preventing competitors, customers and employees knowing the extent of the partnership's profits or losses.

The disadvantages are:

(a) the risk to each partner of personal liability, without limit, for the entire debts of the partnership;
(b) the difficulty of raising a loan against the value of any assets other than heritage.

In practice the main disadvantage of a partnership is that each partner is jointly and severally liable for the debts of the partnership, which means that the partners could potentially lose all their assets and be sequestrated in the event of the insolvency of their partnership.

Limited partnerships
A partnership is not the same as a limited partnership. Limited partnerships are regulated by the Limited Partnership Act 1907, and share characteristics of both limited companies and partnerships. They are registered in the same manner as limited companies, though under their own legislation. In a limited partnership there is a limited partner, who contributes some capital, whose liability to the partnership is limited to that amount of capital and no more (s.4(2)), but who takes no part at all in the management on pain of becoming personally liable (s.6(1)); and there is the general partner who bears all the risk (s.4(2)) and depending on the terms of the partnership agreement obtains a certain amount of the profit less the sums due to the limited partner. An ingenious method of limiting the severity of the risk for either the limited or the general partner is for each partner to be a limited company.

Limited liability partnerships
These were introduced in 2000, and are discussed at the end of the Chapter on companies. They are not the same as either partnerships or limited partnerships.

Rules for determining the existence of a partnership
The significance of being a partner is that not only is a partner normally entitled to the partnership's profits, but he will also be liable for the partnership's losses. It will therefore be in some persons' interests to claim that they are not partners, and hence not liable for losses, when in reality they should be liable. In the absence of a partnership agreement, the following criteria, as delineated in PA, s.2, are used to establish the existence of a partnership:

(a) joint tenancy or joint ownership, irrespective of any profits engendered by the joint tenancy or ownership, does not of itself mean that a partnership is in existence (PA, s.2(1));
(b) the sharing of gross returns (as opposed to profits and losses), even out of any common property, does not of itself mean that a partnership is in existence (PA, s.2(2));
(c) the receipt by a person of a share of the profits of a business is *prima facie* evidence that that person is a partner in the business. This means that the law presupposes that if a person receives a share of the profits he will be a partner. This presupposition may be overturned if other facts show that the person is not to be treated as a partner. Furthermore, PA states that mere receipt of a share of the profits does not automatically mean in every circumstance that the

recipient is a partner. PA, s.2(3) gives five instances where receipt of a share of the profits does not make the recipient a partner, these being:

(i)   the repayment of a debt out of the profits of a business (PA, s.2(3)(a));

(ii) where an employee is rewarded by a share of the profits (PA, s.2(3)(b));

(iii) where the recipient is a dependent of a former partner and receiving by way of an annuity a portion of the business's profits (PA, s.2(3)(c));

(iv) where a lender lends money to a business and the contract for the loan, which must be in writing and signed by all the parties thereto, states that the interest rate is to vary according to the business's profits (PA, s.2(3)(d)); and

(v)   where the recipient is paid an annuity or receives some other benefit out of the profits of the business in consideration of the sale by him of the goodwill of the business (PA, s.2(3)(e)).

As an adjunct to the above, if a person lends money to a business, or if he sells the goodwill of a business to another business (in either case expecting to receive a share of the profits but without necessarily being deemed to be a partner), and if the business goes bankrupt, the lender or the seller of the goodwill, as the case may be, will find that he is treated as a postponed creditor if the borrowing or purchasing business goes into bankruptcy or other form of insolvency. Only once the other creditors have been repaid in full may the lender/seller be repaid (PA, s.3).

RELATIONS OF PARTNERS TO PERSONS DEALING WITH THEM

Liability for partners' acts

Each partner is an agent for the firm, and providing the partner is acting in the usual course of business that his firm practises, his actions bind the firm (PA, s.5). Where the partner does not in fact have the authority to act in a particular transaction, and the person with whom he is dealing either knows that the partner does not have authority for the transaction, or does not know or believe that the partner is a partner, the transaction will not bind the partnership.

This raises the issue of actual and apparent authority, and the extent of the knowledge of the person with whom the partner is dealing. The assumption is that when a partner signs a document on behalf of the partnership he will bind the partnership (PA, s.6), even if as a matter of practice his fellow partners have not permitted him to do so (see *Mercantile Credit Co. Ltd v Garrod* (1962), where an unauthorised partner sold a car contrary to his partnership agreement, and the firm was held bound by his action), unless the matter has been specifically brought to the attention of the contracting party (PA, s.8). If the contracting party's belief in the authority of the partner was unjustified, the partnership will also not be bound (see *Paterson Bros v Gladstone* (1891), where borrowing by one partner, ostensibly on partnership business, of money at an interest rate of 40 per cent could not be construed as acting in the normal course of business). In *Fortune v Young* (1918), a partner guaranteed the financial standing of a young man seeking a tenancy. This was written on partnership headed paper, but it was held that this was clearly a private matter outwith partnership business and the firm was not bound by the letter.

Should a partnership be sued and be unable to meet a decree, technically the debt should be satisfied out of the partnership assets first, and thereafter by the individual partners personally. However, PA, s.4(2) states that where there is a decree against a firm, or diligence levelled against a firm, the creditor may proceed directly against any partner he chooses who is entitled to relief *pro rata* from the firm and the other partners. Partners in a firm are jointly and severally liable for the debts of the firm arising while they are partners: if they die while still partners, their estate then becomes liable in their stead (PA, s.9).

Non-partners may bind the firm in contracts
It is not necessary to be a partner to bind a partnership to a contract. Under PA, s.6 anyone with apparent authority to bind the partnership may do so.

Misappropriation of property by partners
Where an individual partner, or the whole firm, in each case apparently acting within the course of his or its business, receives money from a third party and misapplies it, the firm is liable for the loss (PA, s.11). However, if an individual partner, acting as a trustee, improperly misuses trust property in the firm's business or on account of the partnership, he alone of the partners remains liable for the misapplied property, though any other partner who is aware of the breach by the partner/trustee may still be liable if he has been notified of the partner/trustee's breach, and the property itself may still be recovered from the partnership if it is still in its hands (PA, s.13).

Holding out persons as partners
Where someone purports to be a partner even when he is not, or where a partnership "holds out" or does not contradict the impression that someone is a partner even when he is not, the partnership as a whole will be liable to anyone who lends money to the firm in the belief that the purporting partner is indeed a partner (PA, s.14).

Partners cannot avoid responsibility by claiming ignorance of their fellow partners' pronouncements or by claiming that they have not been informed
Any admission or representation by a partner made in the ordinary course of business about partnership matters may be evidence against the firm

(PA, s.15). This means that if a partner makes an assertion about the firm, he is deemed to have made it on all his fellow partners' behalf, and they cannot pretend to be ignorant of it or assert that his statement was not binding on them.

The converse of section 15 is that a notice to any one partner about any partnership matter is deemed to be notice to the firm as a whole, so that other partners cannot claim that they were ignorant of a matter merely because one of their fellows had failed to communicate the matter to them (PA, s.16).

Vicarious liability of partners

The firm is vicariously liable for any wrongful act or omission of a partner in the ordinary course of business and which causes injury to a non-partner (PA, s.10). In *Flynn v Robin Thompson and Partners* (2000), a partner in a firm of solicitors, in an unusual approach to customer management, saw fit to strike his client. The client was not permitted to sue the partnership since hitting clients was clearly not an act in "the ordinary course of business". Furthermore, where one partner injures another in the course of business, as when one fisherman hurt another with a boathook in *Mair v Wood* (1948), no vicarious liability attaches to the partnership.

The liability of new and retiring partners

An incoming partner is not liable for any debts of the partnership arising from before he became a partner (PA, s.17(1)); a retiring partner remains liable for the debts arising during the period of his partnership (PA, s.17(2)). Normally when a partner retires, the terms of his retirement will clarify what continuing liabilities he will remain responsible for, though as far as outsiders are concerned the retired partner is still liable for the debts arising during his period of partnership. Where a retiring partner has not properly notified third parties of his retirement, he may still be liable as if he were still a partner (PA, s.36(1)), but notice in the *Edinburgh Gazette* serves as notice of retirement to those who have not had dealings with the firm. It does not, however, serve as notice to those who have had dealings with the firm. In theory they need more formal intimation, though in practice this is rarely followed: the usual form of intimation is a change in the partners' names on the headed paper.

THE RELATIONS OF PARTNERS TO ONE ANOTHER

As stated above it is normal and indeed sensible for prospective partners to draw up a partnership agreement. In the absence of an express agreement, agreement may be inferred from the partners' course of dealing (PA, s.19). Partnership property is assumed to be owned by the partnership and each partner is entitled to a *pro indiviso* share, which means that while he may not be easily able to realise partnership property, and creditors cannot effect diligence on the partnership property as a whole if their claim is against the partner in his private capacity, he is entitled on the sale of the partnership property to his proportion of the sale proceeds (PA, s.20). The PA, s.24 outlines the normal rules that will apply to partnerships unless disapplied or varied by the partnership agreement, such as equal division of profits and losses, repayment of partnership expenses, loans to the partnership other than the contribution of partnership capital, interest on the capital, the right to share in the management of the partnership, the prohibition on remuneration for acting in the partnership business, the requirement for the consent of all partners for the adoption of a new partner, the use of the majority vote in deciding partnership business except in the context of changing the partnership business which attracts a unanimous vote, and the accessibility of the partnership books. Partners are in a fiduciary relationship both with each other and with their partnership, so that at all times they must act in good faith in the best interests of the partnership as a whole, without taking any unauthorised advantage of their position (*Finlayson v Turnbull* (1997)).

The PA, s.25 states that no partner may be expelled by mere majority of votes unless the partnership agreement permits this. Section 26 permits retirement at will, subject to any agreement to the contrary.

There is a duty on all partners to render proper and true accounts and to provide true information to each other (PA, s.28). Partners must account to the partnership for any profit deriving from the partnership (PA, s.29) and no partner may compete with his firm (PA, s.30). In *Pillans Bros v Pillans* (1908), one of the brothers and partners in a family firm of manufacturers set up a rival business not far from his family firm. He was required to account to the family firm for his profits from the business. Where a partner assigns his interest in the firm to a third party, the third party has no right of management of that partner's share of the business; instead it merely entitles the assignee to the share of the profits (PA, s.31). It is common for a partnership agreement to prohibit assignation without the consent of the other partners.

DISSOLUTION OF THE PARTNERSHIP

A partnership is dissolved either by the means specified in the partnership agreement, or in the absence of a partnership agreement, by one of the methods stated in PA, s.32, these being the expiry of a designated term, the completion of the undertaking for which the partnership was set up, or by one partner giving notice to the other of his intention to dissolve the partnership. The death or bankruptcy of any partner may also cause the partnership to be dissolved (PA, s.33) unless the partnership agreement says otherwise. Equally, should the partnership be carrying on an illegal activity, it will be dissolved (PA, s.34). The court may dissolve the partnership if the partnership cannot be dissolved by any consensual method, under the PA, s.35, in particular on the occasion of the insanity of a partner, the permanent incapacity of a partner, the misconduct of a partner such that his misconduct would materially affect the carrying out of the partnership business, breach of the partnership business such that the other partners cannot practicably carry on business with him, the partnership making a loss, or where the court considers it just and equitable to dissolve the partnership. Notwithstanding dissolution, the partners remain liable for the debts of the partnership until creditors have been informed of the dissolution of the partnership (PA, s.36), so it is in the partners' interests to notify the dissolution of the partnership as soon as possible: there are mechanisms to permit this (PA, s.37). The partners retain some rights to deal with the partnership property even after the dissolution of the partnership, but only for the purpose of winding up the affairs for the partnership (PA, s.38). The partnership assets are sold or otherwise used to pay the partnership debts, but any surplus remaining after repayment of creditors is divided between the partners on the basis outlined in the partnership agreement or such other basis as may be agreed (PA, s.39). Where the partnership has been dissolved because of the fraud of one or more of the partners, the innocent partner (or partners) is entitled to redress from the fraudulent partners (PA, s.41), and is thereby entitled to a lien over the partnership assets as a method of ensuring his ultimate payment of the sums properly due to him. He is also entitled to be indemnified by the fraudulent partner for any liabilities of the partnership incurred by the fraudulent partner but which had to be paid by the partnership or the innocent partner.

Where a partner dies or retires and the partnership business continues for a while after dissolution as part of the winding up of the partnership, the dead partner's estate or the retiring partner is entitled to his share of the profits or to interest at 5 per cent, unless there is an option available to other partners to buy the dead or retired partners' share (PA, s.42).

Once the partnership assets have been realised, the partnership debts are repaid, first to creditors, then to each partner in respect of advances, next to each partner in respect of his capital and finally the balance is divided up between the partners in the same proportion as profits have been divided up (PA, s.44).

If the partnership becomes insolvent, the Bankruptcy (Scotland)Act 1985 applies to its winding up.

Further reading

Forte (ed.), *Scots Commercial Law* (Butterworths, 1997), Chap.9.
Gloag and Henderson, *The Laws of Scotland* (11th ed., W. Green, 2001), Chap.49.
Mays, *Scots Law: A Student Guide* (T&T Clark, 2001), Chap.10
Pearson and Tyre, "Partnership", *Stair Memorial Encyclopedia* (Law Society of Scotland/Butterworths, 1995), Vol.16.

9. COMPANY LAW

The comparative advantage of the limited company

The major drawback of being a sole trader is his unlimited liability for his debts, and the risk of bankruptcy if his business fails to prosper. The same is true of being a partner in a partnership, except that he bears not only the risk of his own business debts but those of his fellow partners as well.

These two forms of trading may be contrasted with trading through a limited liability company. There are other types of corporation that have limited liability, such as the limited liability partnership (discussed at the end of the Chapter), and there are companies which do not have limited liability, also discussed later. But for convenience sake the main advantages of the limited liability company, relative to sole traders and partnerships, are as follows:

(a) companies have a legal personality separate from those who are employed by it, those who manage it and those who own it;

(b) there is no restriction on the maximum number of members a company may have, though public companies must have a minimum of two, and private companies a minimum of one member;

(c) it is possible to be a member of a company without having to be involved in the management of a company;

(d) a member is not normally liable for the debts of a company beyond the fully paid up value of each share and any premium on the share, unless:

    (i) the member has by a separate undertaking guaranteed the company's debts;

    (ii) the company is a guarantee company in which case he may have to honour his guarantee;

    (iii) the company is an unlimited liability company;

    (iv) the member has been involved in certain fraudulent activities involving the company;

(e) the knowledge that members' liability is limited makes companies more likely to undertake enterprises than they would if members' liability was unlimited. Although this does mean that a company's creditors bear the risk of the company's default, it also means that entrepreneurs are encouraged to set up businesses, thus creating employment and wealth opportunities.

(f) directors, on the whole, are given considerable freedom to manage their companies, and provided they behave reasonably competently, honestly and within the permitted limits of the law are generally able to avoid personal liability for any unfortunate business decisions they make;

(g)   companies may grant security over their assets (including moveable assets) by way of a floating charge; this enables them quickly to raise finance with which to exploit a commercial opportunity;

(h)   companies may raise funds by offering their shares for sale;

(i)   a successful company may offer its shares for sale to the public through a recognised investment exchange, such as the London Stock Exchange, thus creating significant opportunities for wealth, both for entrepreneurs and investors;

(j)   some company directors enjoy the status of being a company director;

(k)   in theory a company may continue indefinitely without ever having to be reconstituted (this being known as "perpetual succession"); even if its members and directors change, the company still remains in existence.

The disadvantages of being a limited company are:

(a)   the company must disclose its accounts and other details on a regular basis—thus revealing information to competitors, creditors and employees;

(b)   most companies' accounts need to be audited at some cost and inconvenience;

(c)   companies must be formed in a prescribed manner; there are costs incurred in incorporation and in complying with the requirements of company law generally;

(d)   it is difficult for an investor to withdraw his capital from the company;

(e)   a'though directors are not normally responsible for their company's debts, in certain instances, such as insolvency, the directors may find themselves liable for the company's debts despite the separate legal personality of the company;

(f)   creditors of small companies often demand personal guarantees from the members or directors, thus removing one of the principal advantages of being a limited company, the freedom from liability for the company's debts.

Many of the above points apply to limited liability partnerships as well. This will be discussed at the end of this Chapter.

THE LEGISLATION APPLICABLE TO COMPANIES

Companies are regulated primarily by:

(a)   Companies Act 1985 ("CA"), which incorporates substantial amendments made by the Companies Act 1989;

(b)   Insolvency Act 1986 ("IA") as amended by the Enterprise Act 2002

(c)   Company Directors Disqualification Act 1986 ("CDDA");

(d) Business Names Act 1985 ("BNA");
(e) Financial Services Act 1986 ("FSA") and the Financial Services and Markets Act 2000 ("FSMA").

THE SEPARATE LEGAL PERSONALITY OF A COMPANY

The separate legal personality of a company has been well established by three cases. (1) *Salomon v A. Salomon & Co. Ltd* (1897). There was no bar to Salomon lending money to his own company and securing the loan by a debenture enabling him to be repaid ahead of other creditors (2) *Lee v Lee's Air Farming Ltd* (1961). The director and majority owner of the company was entitled to contract in his personal capacity as an employee with his own company. (3) *MacAura v Northern Assurance Co. Ltd* (1925). A timber grower transferred the ownership of some timber to a limited company which he controlled. The timber remained insured in his own name. Later he was unable to claim on the insurance policy for the destruction of the timber, as the policy was not in favour of the company.

Lifting the veil
Although the law recognises that a company is a separate legal entity from its owners, managers or employees, there are occasions under common law and under statute where this principle is eroded. This is known as "lifting the veil of incorporation" and enables the court to look at the underlying details of the company. Well known cases under common law where this has arisen include:

  Daimler Co. Ltd v Continental Tyre and Rubber Co. Ltd (1916). In wartime, a predominantly enemy-owned company was forbidden to claim for a debt due to it by a British company.

  Gilford Motor Co. Ltd v Horne (1933). Horne could not avoid the terms of a restrictive covenant by claiming that he was working for a company which was not bound by the restrictive covenant.

  Re FG Films Ltd (1953). It was held that a company which was British in registration but American in every other respect should be treated as if it were a foreign company and taxed accordingly.

  Woolfson v Strathclyde Regional Council (1978). The corporate veil should only be lifted where special circumstances exist indicating that it is a mere façade concealing the true facts. Cases where a "mere façade" has been held to exist include *Re H* (1996) and *Trustor AB v Smallbone* (2001).

Lifting the corporate veil under statute
There are certain occasions under statute where the law will look at the underlying reality of the company or will treat the members or as the case may be the officers of the company as liable for the debts of the company. Some of these are as follows:

(a) IA, s.122(1)(g) (known as the just and equitable grounds)—a quasi-partnership company was wound up following the breach of faith between former partners who had subsequently incorporated their business (*Ebrahimi v Westbourne Galleries Ltd* (1973));

(b) CA, s.117—absence of trading certificate for a public company (as a matter of practice extremely rare) may make the directors personally liable for the company's debts;

(c) CA, s.349—inaccuracy of company name on cheque, etc., makes the signing officer personally liable (*Rafsanjan Pistachio Producers Ltd v Reiss* (1990));

(d) IA, s.213—fraudulent trading by a member or officer of a subsequently insolvent company makes that person liable for the company's debts;

(e) IA, ss. 212, 214—misfeasance or wrongful trading by directors of subsequently insolvent companies makes them liable for the company's debts.

Subsidiaries

In principle a holding company has no liability for its subsidiaries' debts (*Re Southard and Co. Ltd* (1979)).

TYPES OF COMPANY

The two main types of company are private companies and public companies. There are in turn several different types of private company:

(a) unlimited company (rarely used, for the members are personally responsible for the company's debts; no accounts need be published);

(b) guarantee company (commonly used for charities; members are liable for the company's debts up to a guaranteed amount);

(c) private limited company limited by shares (by far the most common);

(d) single member private limited company limited by shares (common for wholly owned subsidiaries).

It is also possible to categorise private companies by financial size, so that there are small companies, medium sized companies and large companies. Certain small companies do not need to provide audited accounts. Neither small nor medium sized companies need produce full accounts.

It is possible to convert an unlimited company into a private limited company, and indeed a private limited company into a public company.

There is only type of public limited company. The principal features of a public company (commonly known as a "plc") are that:

(a) it has a minimum authorised capital of £50,000 and each share must be paid up to the extent of one quarter plus any premium;

(b) the company law rules relating to public companies are considerably stricter and require more disclosure of information and accounts than as is the case with private companies;

(c) a public company could, if it wished, offer its shares to the public.

There is a common misconception that all public companies offer their shares to the public. Some public companies do offer their shares to the public. However, many public companies do not do so: they are merely "public" companies because the more stringent capital requirements and the letters "plc" give the company a credibility and status that it might not otherwise have. However if a company does wish to offer its shares to the public, it must be a public company to do so, for private companies may not issue their shares to the public (CA, s.81).

Companies that wish to offer their shares to the public generally do so on the London Stock Exchange (in which case they are said to be "listed" on the Stock Exchange) or on some other recognised market such as the Alternative Investment Market. In either case, the companies concerned have to comply both with the rigorous disclosure requirements of each market and with the terms of the FSA and of the FSMA.

CORPORATE DISCLOSURE

All companies must disclose information about themselves at the Register of Companies. Failure to send certain documents, such as accounts, to the Registrar of Companies within strict time limits may result in prosecution. Members may also find out about their companies through receiving their annual accounts and directors' reports and may attend shareholders' meetings. There are many complex rules relating to the accounts and capital of a company: these must be followed closely and the accounts and any changes to the company's capital must be properly disclosed to the members and the Registrar of Companies.

The incorporation of a company

In order to incorporate a company, a company needs to provide certain documentation for the Registrar of Companies, these being Form 10 (the initial statement of directors, shareholders, company name (which must not be contrary to BNA) and registered office), Form 12 (the statutory declaration endorsing Form 10), the memorandum of association, the articles of association, and the registration fee. A company's memorandum of association is a public document stating amongst other things the company's name and principal trading activity. A company's articles of association are its internal constitution, detailing how shares may be transferred, directors appointed, meetings held, the rules attaching to different classes of shares, etc. Most companies' articles are based on a template known as Table A, though few companies adopt Table A in its entirety, most altering it to some extent to suit their particular requirements (see, for example, *Bushell v Faith* (1970), where weighted voting was declared to be acceptable) providing that the alteration does not contravene any other rule of law. Companies should stay within the limits imposed on themselves by the memorandum and articles of association, and there are mechanisms to enable members of a company to force the directors to adhere to the company's own rules as laid out therein (CA, s.35).

Equally, members, on joining a company, must accept the terms of the memorandum and articles as they form part of the effective contract between the member and the company as to the terms on which the members hold their shares in the company (CA, s.14) (*Hickman v Kent and Romney Marsh Sheepbreeders Association* (1915)). Classes of shareholders are able to protect their own interests by the rule that states that only the members of those classes may vote on any change to their rights; it is not possible for non-class members to rewrite the class-members' rights (CA, s.125). If the members generally do not like the wording of the memorandum or articles, they may change most elements within the memorandum and articles by means of a special resolution of the members (CA, ss.4, 9).

THE MANAGEMENT OF A COMPANY

Directors

The company is managed by its directors. They are given authority to deal with the commercial and administrative affairs of the company (Table, art.70), subject to some powers of management (such as dismissing the directors under CA, s.303) being retained by the members. It is possible to be a member and a director simultaneously. As directors know better than anyone what is taking place within their company, there are extensive rules, both under common law and under statute (CA, ss.311–347), to prevent directors taking unauthorised advantage of their position within the company unduly to benefit themselves. Directors have a fiduciary duty to act in good faith in the best interests of the company as a whole without taking any unauthorised advantage of their position (*Boston Deep Sea Fishing Co. Ltd v Ansell* (1888)). Where they fail to do so, they will be required to make good any loss to the company or repay any unauthorised profit. Negligent directors have a duty of care to the company and will be required to make good any losses to the company (*Dorchester Finance Co. Ltd v Stebbing* (1989)).

Liability of directors to creditors of the company

Normally a director is not personally liable to creditors of the company, even when the director has acted negligently, provided he has acted through the company (*Williams v Natural Life Health Foods Ltd* (1998)). But where a director instructs or carries out a fraud through his company he cannot avoid personal responsibility for his fraud, as far as his company's creditors are concerned, by claiming that, since he acted through his company, only his company should be liable (*Standard Chartered Bank v Pakistan National Shipping Corporation* (2002)). Directors of insolvent companies may also be required to make good any losses to the company under IA, ss.212–216.

Relief for directors who breach their duties to the company
Under CA, s.727 where a director has breached his duty to the company, it is open to the courts to relieve him of some or all of his liability provided he has acted honestly and reasonably (*Re D'Jan of London Ltd* (1994)).

Disqualification of directors
Directors who abuse their status as directors or who commit certain criminal acts may be banned as directors for up to 15 years by the CDDA where their conduct as a director merits disqualification.

Company secretary and auditor
The *company secretary* ensures that the company complies with all its legal requirements such as organising meetings and sending documents to the Registrar of Companies. He or she is often an accountant, lawyer or chartered secretary.

The *auditor* is required to check the company's accounts before they are lodged with the Registrar of Companies. His report on the accounts should state that the accounts present a "true and fair" view of the company's financial state.

COMPANY BORROWINGS

A company may borrow just like any other legal person. The common name for the document outlining the terms of a loan to a company is a debenture or bond. A company may grant charges over its property as security for the loan. Such charges must be registered with the Registrar of Companies. For further details, see the Chapter on Rights in Security.

SHARES

A share is a unit of ownership in a company owned by a shareholder, and is commonly designated as having a nominal or notional (but not market) value of £1.00. The nominal value of a share is the amount that must be paid by a shareholder to subscribe for a share from the company in order to avoid any further liability to the company. The ownership of shares is commonly evidenced by a share certificate. Shareholders are commonly entitled, amongst other things, to a dividend out of the company's profits (if declared), a right to vote at meetings, to see the accounts and directors' report and to a return of capital on solvent liquidation of the company. A company may have many different classes of shares, each with differing rights and obligations, such as non-voting shares, preference shares, convertible shares, redeemable shares, etc. The total nominal value of the company's shares is known as its share capital. Under what is known as the capital maintenance rule, the share capital is supposed to be a fund of last resort for the benefit of the creditors (sometimes being known as "the creditors' buffer") and funds may only be extracted from the company's share capital following complex procedural rules. These rules preclude the reduction of the company's capital, financial assistance for the purchase of a company's shares, certain dividend payments and repurchase or redemption of a company's shares except under certain tightly controlled circumstances designed, at least in theory, to protect creditors.

Shareholders' meetings

Most companies must have annual general meetings ("AGMs") at which the directors explain the accounts and highlight the future direction of the company. The members may vote on any resolutions that require their assent. Shareholders' meetings are designed to make directors accountable to the members, although this does not always happen in practice. Nonetheless meetings form an admirable opportunity to embarrass directors who have failed to exercise their responsibilities usefully. Members may vote on resolutions, the type of resolution varying according to the significance of the issue:

(a)   special resolutions require the approval of 75 per cent of the voting members and 21 days' notice: they are used for major matters relating to the capital of the company or its constitution;
(b)   ordinary resolutions require a bare majority and 14 days' notice and are used for lesser matters such as removal of directors and the approval of directors' contracts;
(c)   extraordinary resolutions require 75 per cent approval but only 14 days' notice and are used to put a company into voluntary liquidation or for classes of shareholders to vary their rights.

It is possible to have written and elective resolutions in private companies.

CORPORATE INSOLVENCY

Liquidation

A liquidator is a person who is appointed either by the creditors or the members to wind up the company, in other words to sell the company's assets or otherwise turn the company's assets into cash which is then divided up between the creditors. A winding up may be either compulsorily ordered by the court (IA, s.122) because of the company's inability to pay its debts (IA, s.122(1)(f)) or because it would be just and equitable to do so (IA, s.122(1)(g)), or voluntarily agreed upon by the members (IA, ss.84–116). A members' voluntary liquidation means that the company is solvent and can pay its debts in full; a creditors' voluntary liquidation anticipates that the company is insolvent, in which case preferential creditors are paid in full first if possible, then ordinary creditors if there are sufficient funds to distribute to them. Where assets are subject to a charge, such as a standard security over heritage, or a floating charge over moveables, the liquidator is only entitled to deal with the surplus, if any, of the value of the assets over the extent of the charge. A liquidator follows substantially the same rules as does a trustee in bankruptcy and has the same powers to swell the estate by setting aside antecedent transactions, and to equalise diligence, all with a view to maximising the sums due to the creditors. It is open to him to reduce gratuitous alienations (IA, s.242), unfair preferences (IA, s.243), extortionate credit transactions (IA, s.244) and certain floating charges which may have been granted in order to defraud creditors (IA, s.245). Where directors have misapplied company assets (IA, s.212), or where fraudulent trading (IA, s.213), wrongful trading (IA, s.214), or trading through a phoenix company (IA, s.216) have been taking place, the liquidator may apply to the court to make the directors accountable to the company.

Receivership
This is a mechanism by which a secured creditor enforces his rights against a company under a floating charge. It is discussed in detail in the Chapter "Rights in Security" to which reference should be made.

Administration
This is a method of attempting to preserve an ailing company as a going concern in the interests of all the company's creditors generally. During administration a company's affairs are run by an insolvency practitioner and the directors demit office. During administration a company is insulated from its creditors and no steps may be taken by creditors to enforce their rights against the company. Administration is designed to ensure a more satisfactory resolution of a company's financial difficulties than the drastic steps of liquidation or receivership. Administration may take place at the instance of the company, the directors, or its creditors. Following the passing of the Enterprise Act 2002, holders of floating charges granted after the passing of that Act may only appoint administrators (rather than receivers) if they wish to enforce their rights under the floating charges. This should enable all creditors, not just the floating charge holder, to salvage something out of the company's potential or actual insolvency. For further details about administration, see the end of the next Chapter.

LIMITED LIABILITY PARTNERSHIPS

Limited Liability Partnerships ("LLPs") were introduced into the UK by the Limited Liability Partnership Act 2000 ("LLPA"). LLPs share many features of companies, such as:

(a) the separate legal identity of the LLP (LLPA, s.1(2));
(b) requirements of registration with the Registrar of Companies (LLPA, ss.2, 3);
(c) the uniqueness of the LLP's name (LLPA. Sch., Part I):
(d) the need for a registered office (LLPA, Sch., Part II);
(e) the ability to grant floating charges (CA 1985, s.462);
(f) disclosure of accounts and other documentation (Limited Liability Partnership Regulations 2001 (SI 2001/1090) Part II);
(g) insolvency provisions (The Limited Liability Partnership (Scotland) Regulations 2001 (SI 2001/128) Part III);
(h) members acting properly in the course of the business of the LLP are not normally liable for the debts of the LLP (as with directors of companies).

Other features of LLPs are that:

(a) the owners of the LLP are known as "members" (not partners or shareholders). Some members are called "designated members" and they have the task of ensuring that the LLP documentation complies with all necessary LLPA legislation (LLPA, ss.4-6). Members may not transfer their membership in the way that shareholders transfer their shares. Membership is therefore not tradeable.
(b) each member is an agent for the LLP (LLPA, s.6).
(c) IA, s.214A provides that where an LLP has gone into insolvent liquidation, under certain circumstances the liquidator may apply to the court for an order to make a member return to the LLP any assets (including salary) improperly withdrawn from the LLP in the past two years (the "clawback" provision).
(d) the capital maintenance rules do not apply to LLPs.
(e) LLPs do not have a partnership agreement or memorandum and articles of association but they normally will have some internal document which will lay out the rights and duties of the members between themselves. If there is no such document, paras 7 and 8 of the Limited Liability Partnership Regulations 2001 provide a standard set, rather in the same manner as the Partnership Act 1890 does for partners.
(f) LLPs are not obliged to have AGMs or any other members' meetings.

The significant benefit of an LLP is that an LLP is able to keep some of its internal arrangements secret (as with a partnership) while the members have the benefit of limited liability (as with a limited company). The main disadvantage is the requirement to publish accounts.

Further reading

Davies, *Gower's Principles of Modern Company Law* (6th ed., Sweet & Maxwell, 1997).
Gloag and Henderson, *The Law of Scotland* (11th ed., W. Green, 2001), Chap.50.
Grier, *Company Law* (W.Green, 2002).
Sealy, *Cases and Materials in Company Law* (7th ed., Butterworths, 2002).

---

10. RIGHTS IN SECURITY

A lender will seek security for a loan because by doing so he has a better chance of getting his loan back, and the interest thereon, than if he lends the money on an unsecured basis.

If, in addition to having security over a borrower's assets, the lender can have first right to the proceeds of sale of those assets, even when the borrower becomes insolvent, the lender is in an even better position. Indeed, unless he has that right, he may charge a high rate of interest, refuse to lend or, in the case of a limited company, demand extensive personal guarantees from the directors of the company.

There are two main types of security in Scots law: a "real right" (*ius in re*), which give the security holder a right in an item of property, and a "personal right" (*ius in personam*), which is a right against a person to make him carry out some obligation. If that person is insolvent, the right is usually worthless.

Ius in re
A real right gives a creditor a right in the property itself which, generally speaking, cannot be defeated by others' interests. Even if the debtor becomes insolvent the creditor may still have a right in the property.

The type of real right depends on (a) what the property is and (b) who the debtor is. As regards (a), property in Scotland is divided into three main categories, these being: heritable property (effectively land and buildings, in England called "real estate"), also known as "heritage"; corporeal moveable property (tangible assets that can be taken from place to place, such as vehicles and machinery); and incorporeal moveable property (shares, royalties, book debts and other items which though commonly evidenced by paper documentation have no tangible existence).

All legal personae may grant security over any of the assets in (a). As regards (b), certain corporations, being companies registered under the Companies Acts and limited liability partnerships, may have a further type of security normally unavailable to other legal personae, this being a floating charge, which covers not only present assets, but also future assets as they may be from time to time, and which becomes a fixed charge on the occurrence of certain events. Floating charges will be dealt with in detail later.

The significance of delivery

Historically the Scots law on security is derived from Roman law: *traditionibus, non nudis pactis, transferuntur rerum dominia*—by delivery alone, and not merely by agreement, is the ownership in things transferred. If the asset (being the subject of the security) is safely delivered into the lender's hands, there is no doubt as to the strength of the security—as when a pawnbroker retains a debtor's goods until the debt is repaid. As delivery to the lender of an item that will be subject of a security is not always either feasible or commercially desirable nowadays, the law has had to devise stratagems to ensure that the lender's rights are preserved, even when the object of the security is physically immoveable, such as heritage, or in practical terms is bulky or difficult to identify.

SECURITY OVER HERITAGE

As it is clearly impossible physically to deliver land, security over heritage is now effected by drawing up a contractual security document (a "standard security") between the lender and the borrower and subsequently registering it in the Register of Sasines or the Land Register. This is the Scottish form of what in England is known as a (land) mortgage. On its registration the lender obtains a real right in the heritage and becomes known as a "heritable creditor", or sometimes as a standard security holder. The law relating to standard securities is to be found in the Conveyancing and Feudal Reform (Scotland) Act 1970 ("CFRSA"), which sets out the procedure for their registration, standard styles for the wording of standard securities (Sch.2) along with standard conditions that are incorporated into all standard securities (Sch.3). These conditions protect both the heritable creditor and the property owner and include the heritable creditor's right to repossess, sell or foreclose on the property, as well as the rights of the property owner to redeem his standard security and thus have it discharged. There are also provisions to ensure that the property owner is treated fairly and that if any surplus arises out of the sale of the secured assets, the surplus is made over to him. The property owner's rights (and indeed his tenants' rights) are also further protected by the Mortgage Rights (Scotland) Act 2001.

The advantage of the standard security

The advantage of the standard security is that it is a "fixed" charge and that it defeats all other rights. If the owner of the property is sequestrated, and any secured heritage has to be sold by the trustee in sequestration (or the heritable creditor as the case may be), the heritable creditor is entitled to the proceeds of the sale of the property in priority to all other creditors. Furthermore, even if he is solvent, the owner cannot sell the property without first obtaining the standard security holder's consent to the discharge of the standard security—which will generally only be obtained by repayment of any loan secured over the heritage.

Ranking of standard securities

It is possible to have more than one standard security over the same piece of heritage. Normally the order of priority of the securities will be the date order in which they were registered, unless that order is varied by means of a ranking agreement. In the absence of a ranking agreement, when a second security holder registers his security, the first security holder has his security limited to the sums already advanced or required to be advanced in terms of the security documentation, together with interest and expenses (CFRSA, s.13(1)). Where there are floating charges (see later), they will normally be postponed to any properly registered standard securities (Companies Act 1985, s. 464(4)), unless there is some agreement to the contrary (CA, s.464(1A)).

SECURITY OVER CORPOREAL MOVEABLES

As indicated earlier, delivery or its equivalent is required for effective security. As regards moveable items, the simplest method is known as pledge, which is the physical handing over of an asset to the security holder. It may not always be physically possible to hand over the goods, so effective delivery is possible. In *West Lothian Oil Co. (in liquidation) v Mair* (1892), barrels of oil were placed in a locked and fenced off part of a yard and the security holder given the key: this was held to be a satisfactory form of security. Constructive delivery is similar, but as indicated in *HD Pochin & Co. v Robinows & Marjoribanks* (1869), (a) the goods must be genuinely in the hands of an independent third party, not the debtor or his agent, (b) the third party must be informed that he holds the goods on behalf of the security holder, (c) the secured goods must be ascertained and identifiable, and (d) the debtor must have no continuing right to dispose of the goods, except as the creditor's agent (*North-Western Bank Ltd v Poynter, Son and Macdonalds* (1894)).

Symbolic delivery is permissible where the goods themselves do not easily lend themselves to unnecessary warehousing and, by convention, it is accepted that the pledge of a bill of lading is equivalent to the pledge of the goods themselves (*Hayman & Son v McLintock* (1907)). Likewise, a mercantile agent may pledge goods using the documents of title to those goods (Factors Act 1889, s.3).

Normally with a pledge the terms of the pledge documentation allow the creditor to sell the pledged goods, but if such a term is absent, the creditor may apply to court for warrant to sell the goods (Bell, *Principles*, §207).

Pawnbroking is a form of pledge and is extensively regulated by the Consumer Credit Act 1974, ss.114–122.

LIEN

A lien arises when a creditor has possession of the debtor's goods and will not release them until the debtor has fulfilled his obligations to the creditor—as when a garage will not release a car until the repair bill is paid. The right of lien does not automatically give the creditor the right to sell the goods: an application to court would be necessary for that to take place, except (a) under the unpaid seller's lien arising from the Sale of Goods Act 1979, s.39, whereby an unpaid seller may, after giving reasonable notice, resell goods that have not been paid for even where the property in the goods has passed to the buyer, and (b) an innkeeper's lien whereby if a guest has not paid his bill, his retained goods may be auctioned after a period of six weeks (Innkeeper's Act 1878).

HYPOTHEC

A landlord's hypothec is a form of security for one year's worth of rent. Nowadays it is mostly used for commercial subjects, though it may be used for agricultural land not exceeding two acres in size. The landlord may retain the tenant's goods and following a particular court procedure, known as sequestration for rent, he may sell the debtor's assets. The exercise of the landlord's hypothec is not permissible in domestic dwelling-houses (Debt Arrangement and Attachment (Scotland) Act 2002 s.60).

SHIPS AND AIRCRAFT

It is possible to grant a security (without either delivery to or possession by the creditor) over a ship or an aircraft by means of a ship or aircraft mortgage, registrable respectively under the Merchant Shipping Act 1894 and the Civil Aviation Authority. Companies granting such mortgages will also need to register them with the Registrar of Companies (Companies Act 1985, s.410(4)(d)).

RETENTION OF TITLE

Retention of title is a method whereby a seller retains the ownership of an asset until the purchase fulfils some obligation, commonly to pay the purchase price. It is not a true security and is perfectly valid under the Sale of Goods Act 1979, ss.17 and 19, even for all sums due from any other transactions between buyer and seller (*Armour v Thyssen*

Edelstahlwerke AG (1990)). Under the Sale of Goods Act 1979, s.25, a seller's rights may be defeated by a subsequent purchaser acquiring the seller's goods in good faith.

ASSIGNATION

Assignation is the method of effecting a security over incorporeal moveable property such as book debts, royalties, copyrights, proceeds of an insurance policy, rents, etc. The assignor, who is the person entitled to the benefit of the book debts, normally completes a deed of assignation in favour of the assignee, a copy of which is intimated by recorded delivery to the debtor, thus telling the debtor that he must henceforth pay the assignee instead of the assignor. Without intimation to the debtor, any person who establishes a right in the asset, such as a person arresting book debts in the hands of the debtor, will have priority over the assignee.

Assignation is normally done in writing, and there are suggested styles in the Transmission of Moveable Property (Scotland) Act 1862, along with methods of intimation. At the expiry of the period of assignation, the asset is retransferred, or more properly "retrocessed" , to the assignor and the relevant documents returned to him.

Security over shares

A creditor wishing to obtain security over a debtor's shares in a company must arrange for the debtor to transfer the shares to the creditor using a stock transfer form and intimate the transfer to the company. The creditor, having received the new share certificate for the shares, will issue a back letter undertaking to re-transfer the shares to the debtor on the expiry of the underlying obligation for which the security was granted. If the debtor defaults on his obligation, the creditor can sell the shares. A deposit of share certificates with a creditor, while undoubtedly inconveniencing a debtor, does not form an effective security in Scotland, although it does create an equitable mortgage in England.

The defeat of the security holder

Although the whole point of being a secured creditor is to place the creditor in a better position than other creditors in the event of the debtor's insolvency, there are occasions under bankruptcy law when this does not take place. If a debtor attempts to place a creditor in a better position than he would otherwise have been, by means of a security, whether that security be a standard security, assignment or any other form of security, that security may be reduced by (amongst others) a creditor or the trustee in sequestration, if it is established that the security was in fact a gratuitous alienation in terms of either the Bankruptcy (Scotland) Act 1985, s.34 or the common law, an unfair preference under the Bankruptcy (Scotland) Act 1985, s.36, a fraudulent preference under the common law, or part of an extortionate credit transaction under the Bankruptcy (Scotland) Act 1985, s.61. There are similar provisions under the

Insolvency Act 1986, enabling liquidators to reduce the above transactions for corporations. Liquidators may be able to set aside certain floating charges under the Insolvency Act 1986, s.245.

COMPANIES AND LIMITED LIABILITY PARTNERSHIPS

Companies (which in this context also includes limited liability partnerships) also may wish to borrow money and need to grant security for their borrowings. What distinguishes a company from other legal personae in this respect is that companies have to register with the Registrar of Companies most of the securities that they grant. Under the Companies Act 1985, s.410, the under-noted types of security (more commonly known as "charges" in the context of companies) must be registered within 21 days of their creation:

(a) charges over land or interests in land (effectively standard securities);
(b) security over the uncalled capital of a company (very rare in practice nowadays);
(c) security over the following types of incorporeal moveable property, being:
  (i) book debts of the company;
  (ii) calls made but not paid for;
  (iii) goodwill;
  (iv) patents or licences under a patent;
  (v) trademarks;
  (vi) copyrights or licences under a copyright;
(d) securities over ships or aircraft or any share in a ship; and
(e) floating charges (to be discussed later).

The period of 21 days runs from the date of creation of the charge, which is normally the date of execution of the charge by the company, but in the case of a standard security is 21 days from the date of registration of the standard security in the Register of Sasines or the Land Register. Failure to register the charge within 21 days requires a petition to court for late registration (Companies Act 1985, s.420). The danger of failing to register the charge in time is that after the 21-day period of grace, a creditor, liquidator or administrator will be able to defeat the rights of the apparently secured creditor, who will find that instead of being a secured creditor with a prior right to the company's assets over which the security has been granted, he has no such rights and is treated as an unsecured creditor. As proof of the registration of a charge, the Registrar of Companies issues a certificate of registration of charge.

Companies must also keep their own register of charges in addition to the list of charges registered at the Registrar of Companies.

Ideally companies should also register memoranda of satisfaction which are the formal notifications of discharges of charges (Companies Act 1985, s.419).

FLOATING CHARGES

Floating charges derive from English law and form a security which is said to float or hover over the assets of a company, present and future, however constituted. With a floating charge there is no requirement to deliver the asset to the creditor—which means that the company can continue to use the secured assets. The floating charge is based on the expectation (usually enforced in the contractual arrangements between the company and its floating charge holder) that the company will always have enough by way of assets to repay the obligations due to the floating charge holder.

Receivership for pre-Enterprise Act 2002 floating charges

Providing the company performs its obligations to the floating charge holder, the floating charge will continue to float peacefully over the company until the company's debt to the floating charge holder is repaid and the floating charge discharged. Should, however, the company fail to adhere to the terms of the contractual agreements between the company and the floating charge holder and/or

(a) fail to repay the whole sum secured by the charge within a period of 21 days of being asked to do so (Insolvency Act 1986, s.52(1)(a));
(b) have two months' interest in arrears (Insolvency Act 1986, s.52(1)(b));
(c) be wound up either compulsorily or voluntarily (Insolvency Act 1986, s.52(1)(c)); or should
(d) any other floating charge holder appoint a receiver (Insolvency Act 1986, s.52(1)(d)),

the floating charge holder may appoint a receiver, this process being known as "attachment" or more commonly as "crystallisation of the floating charge". In effect what happens is that the charge which had hitherto floated above the company descends upon the company and is then treated as a fixed charge. This means that no other creditors (unless they have a prior right to the relevant assets) may seize those assets instead. The receiver then has various options by way of recouping the loss due to the floating charge holder: for example he may keep the company trading until the debt is repaid; or he may sell the company or parts of it. The receiver's primary interest is to repay the floating charge holder, and while he must be mindful of other interests such as other creditors, he is ultimately working for the benefit of the floating charge holder. In so doing he will ingather certain funds, and out of these he must take account of certain creditors with rights in priority to the charge holder's rights (Insolvency Act 1986, s.60). This may be done either by letting them exercise their rights themselves or he may pay them out of the sums he ingathers. These creditors are creditors with a prior fixed charge of the assets in receivership, creditors who have effectually exercised diligence over the company's assets, the receiver's own creditors in the course of the receivership, the receiver's own fees and expenses, and finally the preferential creditors referred to in the Insolvency Act 1986, Sch.6, these being, amongst other things, certain Government taxes and payments to employees.

It is important to note that a receiver may not seize assets that belong to a third party, as with goods that are being used by the company but are on hire purchase or subject to a retention of title clause.

The anomalous position of a floating charge over heritage
It is not necessary to register a floating charge in the Register of Sasines or the Land Register, yet if the company has heritage, the floating charge on crystallisation acts as if it were changed into a standard security, to the extent of any part of the heritage that is not already subject to a prior-ranking security. However, following the controversial case of *Sharp v Thomson* (1997), where purchasers of a house had paid the purchase price for that house to a company that later went into receivership, and where the purchasers had not at the time of the receivership actually had the disposition in their favour recorded in the appropriate land register, the purchasers were permitted to keep the house and defeat the receiver by the effective creation by the House of Lords of a new type of right, loosely called a beneficial right. The House of Lords' decision on this matter, which overturned the conventional view of a receiver's powers, has been much criticised. Subsequent improvements in conveyancing practice render it unlikely that the issues in *Sharp v Thomson* will arise again, but the legal principle remains the same: where there is an unrecorded disposition but the purchasers have already paid the price on the basis of concluded missives, the receiver's right to the heritage is defeated by the purchasers' beneficial rights to the heritage.

Ranking of floating charges
Floating charges rank in date order of priority unless there is a ranking agreement to the contrary (Companies Act 1985, s.464(1)). As indicated above, floating charges will automatically be postponed to prior-ranking fixed charges (of which standard securities in practice are by far the most common) unless again there is a ranking agreement to the contrary.

The defeat of the receiver
A receiver may not be able to exercise his rights under a floating charge if:

(a) the floating charge was not properly registered (Insolvency Act 1986, s.410);

(b) the floating charge was created within six months of insolvent liquidation and might therefore be an unfair preference under the Insolvency Act 1986, s.243(1), unless it can be clearly established under s.243(2) that the transaction for which the floating charge was created was clearly for value and without any collusive intent;

(c) the floating charge was granted within 12 months of the winding up of the company (or two years if the floating charge holder was a connected person) and the company was insolvent (subject to certain exceptions relating to any benefits given to the company after the creation of the floating charge) under the Insolvency Act 1986, s.245;

(d) the floating charge was granted at any time between the presentation of a petition for an administration order of the company and the granting of that order (Insolvency Act 1986, s.245(3)(c)) or after an administrator has already been appointed (Insolvency Act 1986, s.11(3)(b), (c));

(e) the floating charge was part of an extortionate credit transaction under the Insolvency Act 1986, s. 244;

(f) the circumstances in *Sharp v Thomson* arose.

The effect of the Enterprise Act 2002
This act limits the operation of receivership as delineated above to floating charges created before the implementation of the Enterprise Act. Thereafter floating charge holders having the benefit of floating charges created after the implementation of the Act may only appoint administrators instead of receivers (Insolvency Act 1986, Sch.B1). Although floating charge holders will not need to wait until the company is insolvent to appoint administrators, and although they have certain advantages compared to other potential appointers of administrators, such as only being required to give two days notice of appointment, any administrator, by whomever appointed, will have to act primarily to try to maintain the company as a going concern, which failing the administrator will try to benefit all creditors generally, which in turn failing, the administrator will try to secure the interests of the floating charge holder (Enterprise Act 2002, Sch.16, para.3). The general body of creditors is likely to benefit from the new arrangements, and the Government is renouncing its former right to be a preferential creditor in respect of PAYE and VAT. This is a major change of policy and will result in floating charge holders having considerably reduced powers compared to their former advantageous position. It is anticipated that to compensate for their decreased security many floating charge holders, such as banks, will increase the interest rate on their loans to companies. Alternatively, banks will insist, wherever possible, on fixed charges over company's assets.

Further reading

Forte (ed.), *Scottish Commercial Law* (Butterworths, 1997), Chap.6.
Gloag and Henderson, *The Law of Scotland* (11th ed., W. Green, 2001), Chap.42.
Greene and Fletcher, *The Law and Practice of Receivership in Scotland* (2nd ed., Butterworths, 1992).
Grier, *Company Law* (W. Green, 2000), Chap.15.
Mackenzie Skene, *Insolvency Law in Scotland* (Butterworths, 1999), Chaps 12,13.
Wilson, *The Scottish Law of Debt* (2nd ed., W. Green, 1991), Chaps 7–9.

---

11. BANKRUPTCY

The concept of bankruptcy

Bankruptcy is a legal mechanism for allowing insolvent persons to put a limit on their indebtedness so that they can start afresh in business while giving some redress to creditors.

The meaning of "bankruptcy"

A bankrupt, in ordinary speech, is a person who is insolvent and cannot pay his creditors. A bankrupt may not practise certain professions, such as a solicitor or accountant, and the terms of many employment contracts state that bankruptcy is grounds for dismissal, particularly if the employee is dealing with commercially sensitive matters. A bankrupt may not be a company director or hold certain public offices such as Member of Parliament.

In Scottish legal parlance, the bankrupt is commonly referred to as the *debtor*. The law on bankruptcy is regulated by the Bankruptcy (Scotland) Act 1985 ("BSA") and the old common law. The process of making a debtor bankrupt and having his affairs dealt with by an insolvency practitioner is known as *sequestration*. The person who looks after the affairs of the debtor is known as the *trustee in sequestration*. There are other methods of dealing with a debtor's estate which do not involve sequestration: these include such processes as protected trust deeds and compositions and will be dealt with in due course. Together all the various methods of dealing with an insolvent debtor are known collectively as bankruptcy.

Bankruptcy applies to all legal personae (*i.e.* human beings, partnerships, limited partnerships, trusts, associations and clubs, and certain corporate bodies) (BSA, s.6) but not to registered companies or limited liability partnerships. The equivalent of bankruptcy for those bodies is liquidation.

Bankruptcy is a large and complex subject, and this text does not pretend to do more than give an overview of the major issues and procedures. In particular it does not deal with the insolvent estates of deceased persons. Those who wish to study further are advised to read McBryde, *Bankruptcy*, or Adie, *Bankruptcy*.

Types of insolvency

BSA applies where the debtor is "apparently insolvent", this being occasioned, under section 7, by (amongst other grounds):

(a) the debtor's sequestration in Scotland or bankruptcy in England, Wales or Northern Ireland;
(b) written notice by the debtor to his creditors that he cannot pay his debts in the ordinary course of business;
(c) the granting of a trust deed for creditors (see the end of this Chapter);
(d) the failure to pay a debt after the expiry of the time for payment of a court decree, a registered bond, or Council Taxes or taxes;
(e) failure to pay a debt or debts or provide security amounting to more than £1,500 within a period of three weeks following a valid demand for that sum.

Apparent insolvency ceases when the debt is repaid or when the debtor obtains his discharge.

SEQUESTRATION

Sequestration is the formal process whereby the debtor's estate is put into the hands of a trustee who will then manage or dispose of the debtor's assets in accordance with the rules of bankruptcy. The proceeds therefrom are then distributed among the debtor's creditors. The overall process is supervised and monitored by the Accountant in Bankruptcy.

The Accountant in Bankruptcy

The Accountant in Bankruptcy is an official whose task is to oversee the practice of sequestration in Scotland. He supervises the insolvency practitioners who act as trustees in sequestration or otherwise carry out bankruptcy work, and he himself may be appointed interim trustee or permanent trustee in any sequestration. If either debtors or their trustees commit any criminal acts he may report them to the Lord Advocate for further proceedings.

The outline of sequestration

The outline of sequestration is as follows:

(1) a qualified applicant petitions for the debtor's sequestration;

(2) the court makes an award of sequestration of the debtor's estate;
(3) as part of the award, an interim trustee is appointed;
(4) the interim trustee convenes a first statutory meeting of creditors, on which occasion the permanent trustee is appointed; commissioners may also be appointed to assist him;
(5) the permanent trustee is vested in the debtor's estate, ingathers all the debtor's assets, investigates any relevant antecedent transactions and equalises any diligence;
(6) he then distributes the assets or the proceeds thereof amongst the creditors, taking account of secured and preferential creditors before unsecured creditors;
(7) once the estate is evacuated, the sequestration is terminated, the debtor discharged and the trustee discharged;
(8) as an alternative to the above, it is possible to use the Sch.2 procedure which is a foreshortened version of the above, sometimes known as a small assets case; or
(9) use the Sch.2A summary administration procedure, which is similar to the Sch.2 procedure but falls within certain low financial thresholds.

Who may petition for sequestration?
Under BSA, s.5, the following may petition for sequestration:

(a) the debtor himself with the concurrence of a qualified creditor or creditors (BSA, s.5(2A)) and providing that:
   (i)   the total amount of the debtor's debts is not less than £1,500 (BSA, s.5(2B)(a));
   (ii) there has been no previous award of sequestration within the period of the last five years ending on the date before the date of presentation of the petition for sequestration (BSA, s.5(2B)(b)); and
   (iii) the debtor is either apparently insolvent or has granted a trust deed which was unable to be converted into a protected trust deed because of the valid objections of a creditor (BSA, s.5(2B)(c));
(b) a qualified creditor or creditors provided the debtor is apparently insolvent (BSA, s.5(2)(b)) and providing that the terms of (a) (i), (ii) and (iii) above also apply;
(c) a trustee under a trust deed (BSA, s.5(2)(c)) but only if the debtor has failed without good reason to comply with any term of the trust deed or reasonable instruction to the debtor by the trustee in connection with the trust deed, or when the trustee states in his petition that it would be in the best interests of the creditors that an award of sequestration be made (BSA, s.5(2C)(a) and (b)).

A qualified creditor is one who is due the sum of £1,500 (BSA, s.5(4)). Several creditors may combine so that their joint debt amounts to £ 1,500 or more: they then may collectively sequestrate the debtor (BSA, s.5(2)(b)). For ease of reference both a qualified creditor and a group of creditors who collectively qualify will be known hereafter as a "qualifying creditor".

The timing of the presentation of the petition
The debtor or a trustee acting under a trust deed may petition for a debtor's sequestration at any time (BSA, s.8(1)(a)), and a qualifying creditor may likewise but only where the apparent insolvency on which the qualifying creditor relies was constituted within the preceding four months (BSA, s.8(1)(b)).

Jurisdiction and judicial procedure
Although the Court of Session may hear a petition for sequestration, it is cheaper and more common for the petition to be heard in the sheriff court. The petition is presented to the sheriff in chambers and a "first order" is granted. A copy of the petition is sent to the Accountant in Bankruptcy (BSA, s.5(6)). Where a debtor presents his own petition the first order will be an award of sequestration (BSA, s.12(1)), and the date of sequestration for him will then be the date of the award (BSA, s.12(4)). Where a creditor or a trustee under a trust deed presents the petition, the first order will be a warrant of citation under BSA, s.12(2) requiring the debtor to appear before the court to explain why he should not be sequestrated. In this case the date of sequestration will be the date of the warrant of citation (BSA, s.12(4)(b)). The importance of the date of sequestration is that this is the date from which the debtor's period of sequestration runs, and it may also affect the viability of antecedent transactions.

If the debtor appears in court to present a defence or to explain that the debt for which an award of sequestration was sought has been paid, the court may entertain his defence. If instead the debtor fails to respond to the citation and does not appear, or if the creditor's or trustee's grounds for the petition are justified, the court will make the award of sequestration forthwith (BSA, s.12(3)).

Assuming the award is granted, the sheriff clerk intimates the award to the Register of Inhibitions and Adjudications (BSA, s.14). This means that as from the date of sequestration (at least in theory) the debtor is prohibited from selling his heritable assets. The interim trustee, who will be appointed as part of the award (BSA, s.13(1)), will intimate his appointment in the *Edinburgh Gazette* and will ask creditors to send in their claims to him (BSA, s.15(6)). The interim trustee has the task of safeguarding the debtor's estate for the benefit of the creditors as a whole (BSA, s.2(1)). The interim trustee will either be nominated by the debtor or the creditor, or the Accountant in Bankruptcy may be appointed.

Recall of sequestration
It is possible for the debtor, a creditor, the interim trustee, the permanent trustee or the Accountant in Bankruptcy to petition for recall of an award of sequestration provided the petition for the recall is done within 10 weeks of the date of sequestration (BSA, s.16(4)), or at any time: (a) where the debtor has either repaid in full all his debts or given adequate security for them (BSA, s.17(1)(a)); (b) where a majority of the creditors dwell outside Scotland and it would be more convenient to have the debtor's estate dealt with elsewhere (BSA s.17(1)(b)); or (c) where there are other awards of sequestration or bankruptcy proceeding elsewhere (BSA s.17(1)(c)).

Recall is only available through the Court of Session and if permitted the previous award of sequestration is recalled (BSA, s.17(8)). When an award of sequestration is recalled, it is treated as if it had never taken place, whereas an appeal against an award of sequestration is an appeal on legal grounds against the decision of the courts to make such an award.

The preservation of the debtor's estate
The interim trustee is appointed to safeguard the debtor's estate. The debtor must hand over to the interim trustee all papers, assets and perishable goods (BSA, s.18), and within seven days prepare a list of his assets and liabilities (BSA, s.19). Using the list, the interim trustee will then prepare a preliminary statement of the debtor's affairs which should indicate whether there is likely to be any payment of a dividend to the debtor's creditors (BSA, s.20(1)). The list and the statement are sent to the creditors four days before the first meeting of creditors (BSA, s.20(2)), and if the debtor or his spouse is not forthcoming about his personal finances, the trustee may procure that the debtor or his spouse be required to appear before the sheriff to answer such questions as may be necessary (BSA, s.20(4)). Once the debtor's estate is being managed by the trustee, the trustee may make the debtor complete any transaction (BSA, s.18(2)(e)) or close down his business (BSA, s.18(2)(g)). Equally the interim trustee may apply to the court for permission to keep the debtor's business going in order to make it more marketable later (BSA, s.18(3)(a)(i)).

The first statutory meeting of creditors
The interim trustee must convene a meeting of the creditors within 28 days of the date of sequestration (BSA, s.21), but if the Accountant in Bankruptcy is the interim trustee the period may be extended to 60 days (BSA, s.21 A(1)). There must be seven days' notice of the meeting to every known creditor and the creditors must submit their vouched claims to the interim trustee at or before the meeting in order to be able to vote (BSA, s.22(1)). The interim trustee is chairman of the meeting (BSA, s.23(1)) but must thereupon invite the creditors to elect one of their members chairman in his stead (BSA, s.23(1)(b)) unless no one is willing to act as chairman, in which case he remains chairman. If in the interim

trustee's opinion, as stated in the preliminary statement, there are insufficient funds for a dividend to be paid, he must tell the creditors, who may query his opinion under BSA, s.23(3)(b). If the trustee believes that in view of the small size of the debtor's assets the sequestration should proceed by the Schedule 2 procedure, the interim trustee will intimate as much to the sheriff (BSA, s.23(4)) and the Schedule 2 procedure will then take place. There is no appeal mechanism against the trustee's decision on this matter. A distinctive feature of the Schedule 2 process is that the permanent trustee is not elected, and consequently the Accountant in Bankruptcy, rather than the creditors or commissioners, monitors the trustee's actions.

If the estate falls within the parameters for summary administration (*i.e.* the debtor's assets excluding heritage amount to less than £2,000 and his liabilities excluding sums due under heritable securities amount to less than £20,000), the interim trustee or Accountant in Bankruptcy may apply to the sheriff for a grant of a certificate of summary administration (BSA, s.23A(1)–(3)). This enables the trustee to carry out such work as will benefit the estate but does not require him to take every possible step to ingather the debtor's assets where it would be cost- ineffective to do so. In this case Schedule 2A applies to the duties of the permanent trustee who, as with Schedule 2, is also unelected.

Assuming the debtor's estate is sufficiently large not to warrant the Schedule 2 or Schedule 2A procedure, the creditors will elect a permanent trustee (BSA, s.24(1)) who may be the interim trustee. If there are no creditors present, the interim trustee will inform the sheriff, who will appoint the interim trustee to be the permanent trustee (BSA, s.24(4)) and the Schedule 2 procedure will follow forthwith (BSA, s.24(5)). If the Accountant in Bankruptcy already is the interim trustee, and no meeting is called, or if a meeting is called but no voting creditor attends, or if no permanent trustee is elected, the Accountant in Bankruptcy or his nominee is appointed the permanent trustee (BSA, s.23(3A) and s.25A(1),(2)) and the Schedule 2 or as appropriate the Schedule 2A procedure may follow thereon. The permanent trustee must be an insolvency practitioner (BSA, s.24(2)).

At the first statutory meeting the creditors may elect committee members, known as commissioners, to advise the trustee (BSA, s.30). He is not always obliged to follow their advice and they receive no remuneration or expenses (BSA, s.4). Their role is to supervise the process of realisation of the debtor's estate and to inspect the trustee's intromissions.

The permanent trustee
Assuming there are no objections to the appointment of the permanent trustee, the sheriff on receiving the interim trustee's report on the statutory meeting will confirm the permanent trustee's appointment and issue an "act and warrant" to the permanent trustee (BSA, s.25(2)). The interim trustee is discharged (BSA, s.27).

The permanent trustee is said to be "vested" in the debtor's estate, backdated to the date of sequestration (BSA, s.31(8)). This means that the debtor no longer has any title to the assets in the estate, and equally that the permanent trustee can sign documents such as dispositions and validly transfer title (BSA, s.3(1)). The interim trustee has no such power except in the case of perishable goods (BSA, s.18(2)(c)).

The permanent trustee has considerable powers to dispose of the debtor's estate. His duties are set out in the BSA, s.3, one of them being reporting to the Accountant in Bankruptcy any actions by the debtor which may be criminal in nature (BSA, s.3(3)).

Not all assets of the debtor are vested in the permanent trustee: the trustee has limited rights over acquirenda (as discussed later) or over property which is required for the upkeep and aliment of his family (BSA, s.33(1)(a)). Assets held by the debtor in trust for another do not vest in the trustee (BSA, s.33(1)(b)) and goods subject to a landlord's hypothec for rent as followed up by a sequestration for rent cannot be taken by the trustee (BSA, s.33(2)).

A particular issue has arisen where a debtor, before sequestration, concludes missives for the sale of heritage but the purchaser does not have a recorded title at the time of sequestration. In terms of BSA, s.31(1), and on the analogy of *Sharp v Thomson* (1997), who has better right to the heritage: the trustee or the purchaser? At the time of writing *Burnett's Trustee v Grainger* (2002) is apparently being appealed to the House of Lords in an effort to resolve the position. If *Sharp v Thomson* is not followed, (and many hope that it will not be) on the grounds that sequestration can be distinguished from receivership, the heritage will remain in the hands of the trustee and the purchaser will have a claim against his solicitor for faulty conveyancing.

The position of *acquirenda*

Acquirenda is assets (usually earnings) that the debtor acquires after the date of sequestration, and is deemed to belong to the debtor (BSA, s.32(1)). However, the sheriff may, if necessary, order that a certain amount be deducted from the debtor's earnings to aliment his family and himself (BSA, s.32(2)) and the balance applied to the permanent trustee (see *Brown's Trustee v Brown* (1994)).

Income that a debtor receives after sequestration cannot be touched by diligence arising out of debt due at the date of sequestration (BSA, s.32(5)).

As regards capital coming into the hands of the debtor, if it does so within the period of sequestration, the trustee is entitled to obtain it (BSA, s.32(6)).

Where the debtor has any change in his financial circumstances, such as receiving a large bequest, he is obliged to tell the trustee of these facts and failure to do so is a criminal offence (BSA, s.32(7)).

SWELLING THE DEBTOR'S ESTATE

A major task of the permanent trustee, a trustee under a trust deed or a judicial factor is to maximise the extent of the debtor's estate by examining transactions carried out by the debtor in the period leading up to the sequestration or, as the case may be, the apparent insolvency of the debtor. Such transactions are often known as antecedent transactions. Antecedent transactions may be reduced by the above persons (BSA, s.34(1)(b)), or by a creditor due money in respect of a debt incurred on or before the date of sequestration, or before the granting of a trust deed by the debtor or the debtor's death as the case may be (BSA, s.34(1)(b)). For the purposes of this Chapter and to avoid repetition, any of the above individuals who are entitled to challenge an antecedent transaction will be known as a "challenger". Following a successful challenge, the recipient of an antecedent transaction will be required, under certain circumstances, to return the assets or their value to the debtor's estate, and the assets or their cash equivalent will then be added to the pool of assets distributable to the creditors generally.

Certain of the following antecedent transactions may be challenged both under statute or under common law. Although the common law provisions do still exist and are valid, in practice nowadays only the statutory rules are used, mainly because they are much easier for the challenger to operate. This Chapter only deals with the statutory law. The common law is admirably explained in the article by Mackenzie referred to at the end of this Chapter.

The challengeable antecedent transactions are as follows:

(a) gratuitous alienations (BSA, s.34);
(b) the recalling of a capital sum on divorce (BSA, s.35);
(c) unfair preferences (BSA, s.36);
(d) excessive pension contributions (BSA, ss.36A–36C);
(e) diligence carried out within certain periods relative to the date of sequestration or the onset of apparent insolvency (BSA, s.37 and Sch.7, para.24);
(f) extortionate credit transactions (BSA, s.61).

Reduction of gratuitous alienations under statute
A gratuitous alienation is the Scots term for a gift, the transfer of an asset for no value or less than full value, or the renunciation of a claim or a right (BSA, s.34(2)(a)). It is not unusual for a debtor to give away his assets rather than let his creditors or the trustee seize them. To prevent this abuse a gratuitous alienation is challengeable by any challenger (BSA, s.34(1)) where any of (a), (b) or (c) below have taken place, together with (d):

(a) the sequestration of the debtor's estate (BSA, s 34(2)(b)(i));

(b) the granting of a trust deed which subsequently is protected (BSA, s.34(2)(b)(ii));
(c) the death of the debtor and the sequestration of his estate within 12 months of his death (BSA, s.34(2)(b)(iii));
(d) the alienation took place on a relevant day (BSA, s.34(2)(c)).

A relevant day is the day that the alienation became completely effectual (for example, a standard security is only effectual on registration in the Register of Sasines, not on execution), but it also depends on who the recipient is. If the recipient is an associate of the debtor, the relevant day is any date within a period of five years prior to the date of sequestration, the granting of the trust deed or the death of the debtor (BSA, s.34(3)(a)). An associate is defined in the BSA, s.74 as effectively a close relation, an employer or employee, a partner or a company of which the debtor is a director. If the recipient is not an associate, the period is of two years' duration only.

There are exemptions to the above rule. If the recipient can establish any of the following, the alienation will not be reduced:

(a) at the time of the alienation or at any other time after the alienation the debtor's assets were greater than his liabilities (BSA, s.34(4)(a));
(b) the alienation was made for adequate consideration (BSA, s.34(4)(b));
(c) the alienation was a birthday, Christmas or some other conventional gift (such as a wedding present), or was made for a charitable purpose to someone who was not an associate of the debtor, and it was reasonable to have made the alienation (BSA, s.34(4)(c)).

Where a recipient has sold a gratuitously alienated asset to a third party who acquired it in good faith and for value, the third party is not required to deliver the asset back to the trustee. The recipient instead would have to pay the value of the alienated asset back to the sequestrated estate. This is permitted by the wording of the BSA, s.43(4) which allows the court to grant reduction "for such restoration of property to the debtor's estate or other redress as may be appropriate". It would appear from the case *Short's Trustee v Chung* (1991) that reduction is the preferred remedy and only where that is impossible or inappropriate will some other form of redress be allowed.

If a recipient of a gratuitous alienation receives an asset from the debtor for less than adequate consideration, he still has to return the asset to the debtor's estate, even though he may have paid some money for it, and he may claim against the estate as a creditor in respect of what he did pay—but only as a postponed creditor (BSA, s.51(3)(c)).

The term "adequate consideration" was considered in *McFadyen's Trustee v McFadyen* (1994), where it was held that consideration is to be given its normal meaning, namely that something of material or patrimonial value is paid.

A further exemption arises under the BSA, s.34(7), whereby life assurance policies written under the protection of the Married Women's Policies of Assurance (Scotland) Act 1880 in favour of one's spouse and children are protected from reduction.

It can be seen that anyone receiving an asset from a donor likely shortly to be sequestrated is well advised to pay a proper price for the asset or obtain proof of the donor's solvency at the time of the alienation.

Recalling a capital sum paid on divorce

If a debtor pays a capital sum to his spouse as part of their divorce settlement, and if at the time he was either absolutely insolvent or became so as a result of the payment, and within five years he: (a) is sequestrated; (b) grants a trust deed which becomes protected; (c) dies and within 12 months his estate is sequestrated; or (d) dies and within 12 months a judicial factor is appointed over his estate, the court may make an order recalling the order for the repayment of the capital sum to the estate (BSA, s.35). This may be made by any of the challengers referred to earlier with the exception of creditors.

Unfair preferences

Unfair preferences arise when a debtor wishes to place certain creditors in a better position than other creditors, usually because he hopes to retain the creditors' continued goodwill after his bankruptcy. It is sometimes done by giving a creditor a security for an unsecured debt or by repaying a favoured creditor long before payment is due. Under BSA, s.36(1), an unfair preference may be challenged by any of the challengers as in gratuitous alienations (BSA, s.36(4)) if the preference was created not more than six months before (a) the date of sequestration of the debtor's estate or (b) the granting of a trust deed which becomes protected.

Under BSA, s.36(2), there are certain transactions which are exempt from challenge, these being:

(a) a transaction in the ordinary course of business;
(b) a payment in cash for a debt that was due to be paid, unless the transaction for which the cash was paid was collusive with the purpose of depriving other creditors of funds;
(c) a transaction in which each party undertook reciprocal obligations, either simultaneously or over a period of time, unless as in (b) it was collusive;
(d) the granting of a mandate by a debtor authorising an arrestee to pay over arrested funds to the arresting creditor.

Assuming the challenge is successful the court will reduce the transaction and the subject of the transaction will be returned to the estate (see *Balcraig House's Trustee v Roosevelt Property Services* (1994)) unless some other redress may be more appropriate (BSA, s.36(5)), always providing that the rights of third parties acquiring assets, originally the subject of the unfair preference, in good faith and for value, are protected (BSA, s.36(5)).

It would appear that collusion (see (b) above) requires the involvement of both parties to the collusion. In *Nordic Travel Ltd v Scotprint Ltd* (1980), the creditor, knowing that the debtor was insolvent, wanted payment in cash. Although this might have appeared collusive, it was not so because the transaction in question was in the ordinary course of business and a payment in cash does not automatically imply collusion.

The reciprocal obligation exemption (sometimes known as the *nova debita* exemption) is unobjectionable because the estate is simultaneously losing an asset but receiving some other asset or benefit. Accordingly the overall estate is not deprived of anything (see *Nicoll v Steelpress (Supplies) Ltd* (1992)).

Excessive pension contributions

A debtor might well be tempted to pay large quantities of his money into a pension fund to be held in trust until his retirement. This is now struck at by BSA, ss.36A–36C. These subsections state that the courts can reduce excessive payments into the debtor's pension fund over the five years preceding the award of sequestration and substitute reasonable payments thereto instead (BSA, s.36B).

Equalisation of diligence

Diligence is the process whereby a creditor, with the benefit of a court judgment or certain instruments of debt, may if necessary instruct messengers at arms (for the Court of Session) or sheriff officers (for the sheriff court) to enforce the creditor's rights of payment in terms of the carefully controlled procedure laid down in the Debtors (Scotland) Act 1987 and the Debt Arrangement and Attachment (Scotland) Act 2002 (for the details of which, see the end of this Chapter).

One of the virtues of sequestration is that a debtor's creditors can no longer carry out diligence against him once he is sequestrated (BSA, s.35(2)). However, before a debtor is sequestrated or becomes apparently insolvent, creditors may have been trying to carry out diligence against the debtor, and the more aggressive creditors will normally be repaid first at the expense of other creditors who have been politely waiting their turn. The law of Scotland deems this to be unfair on the less aggressive creditors and treats all creditors carrying out diligence within 60 days before sequestration or 60 days before apparent insolvency (in which latter case the period is also extended by a further four months afterwards) as having all carried out their diligence on the same day ("the equalisation date"). All the seized assets are pooled and the trustee divides up the assets *pari passu* (*i.e.* on a proportional basis) amongst all the creditors. This is known as equalisation of diligence and the law relating to it may be found at BSA, s.37 (where the debtor has been sequestrated) and BSA, s.75(1)(b) and at Sch.7, para.24 (where the debtor is apparently insolvent).

Extortionate credit transactions

Under the BSA, s.61 where the terms on which a debt requires to be repaid are deemed to be extortionate, the court, on the application of the permanent trustee, may set aside the transaction in whole or in part or otherwise, at its discretion, vary the transaction. The creditor would then be required to return any excessive payments to the trustee. It is for the creditor to prove that the terms of the transaction are fair and not extortionate. The transaction in question must have been entered into within three years of the date of sequestration.

MANAGEMENT OF THE ESTATE

The trustee will carry out as necessary the above methods of swelling the estate, but he may if he thinks it appropriate, and with the advice and consent of the commissioners, the creditors and the courts as the case may be, continue the debtor's business to raise more funds with which to pay creditors or may raise court actions (BSA, s.39). Commonly the trustee proceeds to sell as much of the debtor's estate as he is permitted to sell. Where the debtor has heritage over which there is a standard security, either the heritable creditor or the trustee may sell the heritage, but each must account to the other so that the heritable creditor receives his debt in full and the surplus, if any, is handed to the trustee (BSA, s.39(4)). There are also procedures under Schedule 1 to enable the trustee to have the heritable security assigned to him in return for payment of the secured debt. The trustee must have regard to the rights of the debtor's spouse and children (BSA, s.40) and if the debtor or his family believe that the sale of the house is premature, they may apply to the court for a delay in the sale.

Examination of the debtor

Sometimes it is necessary for the debtor to be examined in public or in private, before the trustee or before a sheriff (BSA, ss.44–47). The advantage of a private examination is that a "quiet chat" may reveal more than a more formal examination; the advantage of a public examination is that the presence of creditors, the panoply of the law and cross-examination in the atmosphere of a court room may put pressure on the debtor to reveal what he ought to reveal.

Creditors' claims

Creditors must supply their vouched claims (and indeed will generally already have done so if they attended the first meeting of creditors) which will, if accepted, entitle them to draw a dividend from the debtor's estate (BSA, ss.48–50). Where the trustee rejects a claim, there are procedures available for the creditor to appeal to the sheriff (BSA, s.49(6)). Where a creditor is both due money to a debtor and is due money from a debtor, he may exercise set-off, provided the pre-insolvency debts are kept separate from the post-insolvency debts.

Distribution of estate

The debtor's estate, once fully ingathered, is distributed to the various creditors in the following order of priority (BSA, s.51(1)):

(a) the outlays and remuneration of the interim trustee;
(b) the outlays and remuneration of the permanent trustee;
(c) where the debtor has died, his deathbed and funeral expenses and the expenses of administering his estate;
(d) where a creditor has petitioned for sequestration, the creditor's expenses;
(e) preferred debts (to be discussed shortly);
(f) ordinary debts (*i.e.* unsecured creditors' debts);
(g) interest on preferred debts and on ordinary debts;
(h) any postponed debt.

A *preferred* debt is one of the debts in Part I of Schedule 3 to the BSA and covers certain debts to the Inland Revenue, debts due to Customs and Excise, social security contributions, contributions to occupational pension schemes and certain payments to employees. These creditors are known as the preferential creditors.

Ordinary debts include any debt due to a heritable creditor which was not satisfied by the sale of a property.

A *postponed* debt is either a loan from the debtor to his business where his business is a partnership, or a loan made to the debtor by his spouse, or the value of an asset that formed part of a gratuitous alienation which was challenged by the trustee (BSA, s.51(3)).

It is unusual for an estate to be quickly divided: some bankruptcies take some years to be sorted out and the creditors receive small payments over a period of time. Frequently there are insufficient assets for all creditors to be repaid in full and the ordinary creditors may agree to settle for a percentage of what they are due. The trustee's accounts require to be exhibited to the commissioners and the Accountant in Bankruptcy (BSA, s.53).

If at the end of the day there is any surplus, it is returned to the debtor or his successors (BSA, s.51(5)).

The debtor

After three years the debtor is automatically discharged (BSA, s.54(1)) unless the permanent trustee or a creditor applies to the court to have the debtor's period of bankruptcy extended by up to a further two years (BSA, s.54(4)). Once the debtor is discharged, he is free to be a company director again and to hold public office.

Until the debtor is discharged he is subject, under pain of prosecution (BSA, s.67), to various requirements to inform the trustee of any concurrent proceedings elsewhere and to co-operate with the trustee generally.

Under the Enterprise Act 2002, a debtor in England and Wales is rendered bankrupt for a period of 12 months only, thus creating a disparity with Scots law. It would therefore be advantageous for a debtor to be made bankrupt in England. It remains to be seen whether Scottish insolvency law will need to change its rules to follow the English procedure.

The discharge of the permanent trustee

The permanent trustee may apply for his discharge once he has made his final division of the estate, and assuming the Accountant in Bankruptcy is satisfied with the trustee's accounts and all other documentation including his sederunt book (his record of all transactions and accounts), he will in due course receive his certificate of discharge (BSA, s.57).

ALTERNATIVE METHODS OF DEALING WITH DEBTORS' ESTATES

Compositions

A composition is where the creditors agree to discharge a debtor in exchange for part payment of their debts. It may sometimes arise where a member of the debtor's family agrees to reinvest in the debtor so that by the refloating of his business he may ultimately repay his creditors in full. If this is done judicially it is known as a general composition. The proposed terms are offered to the Accountant in Bankruptcy and, if approved, to the creditors. A dividend of at least 25 pence in the pound must be payable to the creditors if the composition is to proceed. A two-thirds majority (in value) of the creditors must approve the composition and the sheriff is asked to consider and approve the composition. If approved by him the composition proceeds according to its terms (BSA, Sch.4).

Compositions are not greatly used because any creditor who does not approve of the terms of the composition remains free to carry out diligence against the debtor, thus probably making it harder for the debtor to fulfil the term of the composition. If the debtor defaults on his undertakings in the composition, creditors may resume their actions against him.

Schedule 2 procedure

As indicated above, the Schedule 2 procedure is like a simplified version of normal sequestration. It is used where no permanent trustee is elected. The Accountant of Court or his nominee becomes the trustee and he has wide authority to realise the estate in the manner of a permanent trustee.

Summary procedure

In a sequestration it may happen that the extent of the debtor's assets is so small that it is not worthwhile justifying the considerable expense of investigating every claim that the estate might make. Accordingly it is open to a trustee to apply to the court for a certificate of summary administration which permits him to reduce the amount of work to what will be of use to the estate and no more. The trustee may apply for such a certificate where the aggregate amount of the debtor's assets excluding heritage does not exceed £2,000 and the aggregate amount of his debts excluding heritable securities amounts to £20,000 (BSA, s.23A). The duties of the trustee once appointed in terms of the certificate are outlined in Schedule 2A and are broadly similar to the ordinary duties of a permanent trustee, save that the trustee is not required to expend time and money on activities which in his view would be unprofitable for the estate as a whole.

Trust deeds for creditors

A trust deed for creditors was originally a method whereby a debtor could convey to a trust such of his estate as could be agreed upon by all the creditors. The trust would then be administered by the trustee for the creditors. Much depends on the wording of the trust deed, the co-operation of the debtor, and the willingness of the creditors. A trust deed's major failing is that any creditor who does not accede to the trust deed is not bound by it, and may continue with action against the debtor. As this may be vexatious for the other creditors, ordinary trust deeds are rarely used, though it is possible for the trust deeds to be "protected trust deeds" which more effectively safeguard the remaining creditors and the debtor from the predations of the non-acceding creditor.

The protected trust deed

If a trust deed fulfils certain conditions specified in BSA, Sch.5, including the requirement to transfer to a trust the debtor's entire estate with the exception of vital necessities for himself and his family, the trust deed may be "protected". The other conditions are that all known creditors, to whom intimation of the proposed trust deed has been made, must, to the extent of a majority in number or at least a third in value, either assent to the terms of the trust deed or fail to notify the proposed trustee (who must be an insolvency practitioner qualified to be a trustee in sequestration) of their objections within five weeks. If this is done the trust will be protected and the protected trust deed registered with the Accountant in Bankruptcy. Those creditors who have done nothing are deemed to have accepted the deed. A validly objecting creditor has a period of six weeks from the date of the original intimation to apply to the court for sequestration, and the creditor may also apply at any time for the debtor's sequestration if he can prove to the court that the distribution by the trustee is unfairly prejudicial to that creditor's interests. The trustee himself may apply for the debtor's sequestration where the debtor has unreasonably not adhered to the terms of the trust deed or failed to comply with a reasonable instruction from the trustee (BSA, s.5(2C)). The debtor may not apply for sequestration while the trust deed is in operation.

The protected trust deed has proved considerably more popular than the trust deed. The trustee pays out the estate in the same manner as a trustee in sequestration and the whole process may be cheaper, easier, and less embarrassing for the debtor than sequestration. It may even result in a quicker discharge both of the debtor and ultimately of the trustee.

The effect of the Debt Arrangement and Attachment (Scotland) Act 2002

As a potential alternative to bankruptcy, this Act provides a structure to enable a person to settle his debts over a period of time. A debtor in financial difficulties will obtain advice from a specialist "money advisor" in the setting up of a "debt payment programme". The programme needs to be approved by the debtor's creditors and by the Civil Enforcement Commission. During the approval process there is a moratorium on enforcement action by the debtor's creditors. If the programme is approved, the debtor may not obtain any further credit and an approved "payments distributor" will distribute the debtor's funds (including some of the debtor's wages) to his creditors. Programmes are expected to run from three to five years. At the time of writing secondary legislation on the implementation of these matters is awaited.

Further reading

Adie, *Bankruptcy* (Institute of Chartered Accountants in Scotland/W. Green, 1997).
Forte (ed.), *Scots Commercial Law* (Butterworths, 1997), Chap.7.
Gloag and Henderson, *The Law of Scotland* (11th ed., W. Green, 2001), Chap.53.
McBryde, *Bankruptcy* (2nd ed., W. Green, 1995).
McKenzie Skene, *Insolvency Law in Scotland* (T&T Clark, 1999).
McKenzie, "Gratuitous Alienations and Unfair Preferences on Insolvency" (1993) 38 J.L.S.S. 141.

---

12. INTELLECTUAL PROPERTY

THE NATURE OF INTELLECTUAL PROPERTY

Intellectual property is a form of incorporeal moveable property, and has been defined by the World Intellectual Property Organisation as literary, artistic and scientific works, performances of performing artists, broadcasts, inventions in all fields of human endeavour, scientific discoveries, trade marks, service marks, commercial names and designations and all other right resulting from intellectual activity in the industrial, scientific, literary and artistic fields. The law operates to protect and to some degree provide a monopoly for the author, inventor, originator, designer or owner in order to prevent others unauthorisedly or unfairly exploiting the intellectual property owner's rights. Depending on the type of right, these rights either arise automatically or arise on registration in the appropriate register.

Intellectual property rights are now mostly protected through statute and through regulations deriving from European directives, although both directives and legislation struggle to keep abreast of new developments in technology such as the internet.

An intellectual property right owner may exploit his right as he sees fit, including selling it or assigning it in security, but commonly an intellectual property owner will license others to use or share his right on payment of a fee, a rent or a royalty.

Inevitably, this Chapter can do no more than provide a brief overview of the main areas of the law relating to intellectual property.

Copyright

Copyright is the right to prevent others from unauthorisedly copying or otherwise without consent using an author's work. There is no register of copyright as there is of trade marks, but copyright arises on the creation of a work that qualifies as capable of being copyright. Copyright cannot protect ideas, but it does protect the expression, in recordable form, of those ideas unless the idea could only be expressed in the one way, in which case copyright will protect both the expression and the idea (*Ibcos Computers Ltd v Barclays Highland Finance Ltd* (1994)). Copyright is regulated by the Copyright, Designs and Patents Act 1988 ("CDPA") and protects anyone who is British and resident or domiciled within a country covered by the Universal Copyright Convention or the Berne Copyright Convention. Works that may be protected are original literary, dramatic, musical and artistic works, sound recordings, films, broadcasts and typographical versions of these works (CDPA, s.1). This protection covers computer programs and databases (CDPA, s.3) but not names, facts, mathematical theories and titles. Subject to certain exceptions, anyone who wishes to use copyright material must seek permission first from the copyright owner, such permission commonly being obtained by payment of a fee.

Originality

A copyright work need not be novel, but it must be original (*University of London Press Ltd v University Tutorial Press Ltd* (1916)), and it must have involved a degree of "skill, judgement and labour". How much of these attributes are required will depend from case to case (*Biotrading & Financing OY v Biohit Ltd* (1988)). No degree of quality is required (*Kenrick & Co. v Lawrence & Co.* (1890)).

Infringement
If someone breaches the terms of any copyright, by unauthorisedly using or copying the author's work (CDPA, ss.16–27), the copyright owner may obtain an interdict against the infringer, or the infringer may be required to pay damages to the copyright owner and/or deliver the infringing items to the owner (CDPA, ss.96–106). Infringement is also a criminal offence (CDPA, ss.107–114). There are certain defences, amongst them being prior permission by the copyright owner, research and private study (provided it amounts to "fair dealing" (*Hubbard v Vosper* (1972); CDPA, s.29)), literary or other criticism and news reporting (CDPA, s.30), copying done for instruction or examination and for other educational or archiving purposes (CDPA, ss. 32–44).

Duration of copyright
Copyright for literary, dramatic, musical and artistic work endures for 70 years from the date of death of the originator (CDPA, s.12). Other work attracts lesser periods. Paternity and moral rights, which are the rights of an author to an unassignable right to be identified as the author of his work (CDPA, s.77), the right to object to false attribution of his work (CDPA, s.77) and the right to object to derogatory treatment of his work (CDPA, s.80), also endure for 70 years (CDPA, s.79).

Patents
Patents are regulated by Patents Act 1977 ("PA"). A patent is obtained by applying for a patent from the UK Patent Office (PA, s.14). It is also possible to have a patent registered in Europe or elsewhere. Normally applications for both these processes are carried out by specialist patent agents. The whole processing of patenting can take up to four years while the proposed patent is carefully examined (PA, ss.17,18) to ensure it meets the legal requirements of novelty, an inventive step and industrial application (PA, s.1(1)(a),(b) and (c)). Certain items are excluded from patentability: a discovery, scientific theory or mathematical method, a literary, dramatic, musical or artistic work, a scheme, rule or method for performing a mental act, playing a game, a program for a computer, or the presentation of information (PA, s.1(2)). PA, s.1(3) prevents the patentability of matters that would lead to immoral or antisocial behaviour, of animal or plant varieties and biological processes for the production of plants and animals (though see the *Harvard/Oncomouse* case (1990)). Patents endure for 20 years (PA, s.25). A registered patent owner may protect his patent by taking action against infringers in the same manner as a copyright owner: he may obtain an interdict to prevent unauthorised use, he may claim damages and he may require delivery of the infringing items (PA, ss.60–71). There are some defences under PA, ss.72 and 74, such as the item not being patentable in the first place, or being granted to someone who was not entitled to it, or under PA, s.60(5), such as the infringement taking place privately or occurring during

experimentation. There are criminal penalties for infringement (PA, ss.110,111).

The Patent Office has a useful website: *http://www.patent.gov.uk.*

Trade marks

The Trade Marks Act 1994 ("TMA") protects a trader's brand name or identifying symbol and reserves to him the right for ten years (renewable on application) (TMA, s.42) to use his trade marks for his products. A trade mark is described in TMA, s.1 as "any sign capable of being represented graphically which is capable of distinguishing goods and services of one undertaking from those of another". The word "sign" is widely defined and includes diagrams, music, shapes, packaging, words, gestures and even smells. Trade marks are registered in the Trades Marks Registry, part of the UK Patent Office in Cardiff. European applications are dealt with at the European Trade Mark Office in Alicante. As with patents, it is common to apply for registration through specialist trade mark agents. Registrable trade marks must not lack "distinctive character" (TMA, s.3(1)) or in some way serve to create a monopoly on the use of everyday words (TMA s.3(1)). They must not offend public morality or be of such a nature as to deceive the public in some manner (TMA, s.3(3)). Certain internationally accepted symbols, such as the Red Cross, and national and heraldic devices may not be registered without appropriate consent (TMA, s.4). A trade mark owner is entitled to the same remedies on infringement of his trade mark rights as the other intellectual property owners specified above, and may invoke his rights when he discovers that some infringer is using a sign identical to his trade mark, or something similar, in a manner causing confusion on the part of the public arising out of the likelihood of association with the trademark (TMA, s.10), subject to certain permitted defences (TMA, s.11). There are also criminal penalties for infringement (TMA, s.92-95).

Design rights

There are two types of design right: unregistered and registered. Unregistered design rights are protected by the CDPA, ss.213–264 which applies to any aspect of the shape of an item provided that design is original. These rights, however, do not afford protection to methods or principles of construction, features of shape or configuration which enable the article to fit with another article (the "must-fit" exception) or are dependent on the appearance of another article (the "must-match" exception) or surface decoration (CDPA, s.213). The protection is generally for 15 years after the first recording of the design (CDPA, s.216). Registered designs are protected by the Registered Designs Act 1949 as amended by various regulations thereafter ("RDA") and are registered in the Trade Marks Register. European design rights are registered with the European Trade Mark Register. The duration of the protection on registration is five years, renewable up to a period of 25 years (RDA, s.7). Under RDA, s.1 any features of "shape, configuration, pattern or ornamentation", which is new, and which has "individual character" to an "informed user" may be registered. Unlike a patent, there is a period of twelve months during which a design may be tested on the public without losing the novelty criterion. Certain designs may not be registered, these being designs that fail to fulfil the requirements of s.1, that are protected by other means (such as copyright), that are contrary to public policy or principles of morality (RDA, s.3(3)) or that are predicated by their technical function or their requirement to be connected to or match another part of another design (the must-fit, must-match exceptions). The must-fit and must-match exceptions are excepted because the Government does not wish manufacturers to be able to have a monopoly on the provision of spare parts. Both unregistered and registered design rights may be protected against infringement in the same manner as indicated for the other intellectual property rights, with the same remedies and criminal penalties.

Passing off
Passing off is the misuse or imitation of a registered trade mark or other design right by a person not entitled to do so, usually in order to obtain the benefit of the image or quality of the original, or to mislead the public into buying the imitator's products. In *Taittinger S A v Allbev Ltd* (1994) Taittinger successfully prevented Allbev Ltd copying Taittinger's distinctive designs for its bottles.

Further reading
Intellectual property is a very fast moving field with a great deal of legislation coming from Europe. The UK Government's intellectual property portal is very useful: *www.intellectual-property.gov.uk* .

Bainbridge, *Intellectual Property Law* (5th ed., Longman, 2002).
Bentley and Sherman, *Intellectual Property Law* (Oxford University Press, 2001).
Cornish, *Intellectual Property Law* (5th ed., Sweet & Maxwell, 2003).
Hart and Fazzani, *Intellectual Property Law* (2nd ed., Palgrave, 2000).
Holyoak and Torremans, *Intellectual Property Law* (3rd ed., Butterworths, 2000).

APPENDIX: SAMPLE EXAMINATION QUESTIONS AND ANSWERS

These questions are adapted from recent examination questions at the University of Edinburgh and at Napier University, whose permissions for their use is gratefully acknowledged.

1. On December 1, 20X1, Jim informs Angus of Angus Mighty Motors Ltd, a car dealer, that he wishes to buy a tough all-weather four wheel drive vehicle for his remote farm in Argyll. Angus, who has visited the farm, informs Jim that he has a vehicle which in his opinion should be able to cope with the demanding conditions Jim experiences at his farm. The vehicle, known as the Highlander, is new on the market and on Angus's suggestion, Jim takes the vehicle for a test drive through Oban. Jim professes himself satisfied with the vehicle and pays for the vehicle before driving it home to his farm. Just before he leaves, he notices a specialised tow-truck which happens to be very well designed for Jim's other car. As he has been looking for this model of tow-truck for a long time, and as the model has recently gone out of production, he agrees to buy it and pays for it, but tells Angus that he will pick it up when he next brings his other car into Oban. Angus agrees to look after it until then. Jim then drives home, without difficulty, in his new Highlander.

A month later, Jim is driving the Highlander on his farm when it gets stuck in the mud and he has to be rescued. This happens again the following week, whereupon Jim reads in a car magazine that according to tests, the Highlander is an excellent vehicle for rocky tracks but is very unsatisfactory in fields where its weight and its unmanoeuvrability often result in it becoming stuck. Furthermore, the windscreen wipers do not work properly. Jim writes to Angus to ask for his money back, and Angus refuses to let him have it. To add injury to insult, when Jim telephones Angus, Angus inadvertently lets slip that by mistake he had sold the tow-truck to somebody else who had taken it away and he cannot find a replacement. Advise Jim.

This question deals with the Sale of Goods Act 1979 ("SOGA") and in particular with section 14 (implied term about satisfactory quality). There are various issues arising from the question, amongst which are fitness for the purpose for which the vehicle was acquired, the opportunity given to Jim to inspect the vehicle, the sale by the seller in possession and the unsatisfactory quality of the wipers.

It is clear that Jim had made known to Angus the particular purpose for which he wished to use the vehicle, and that under SOGA, s.14 there is an implied term of the contract between Jim and Angus that the vehicle will be reasonably fit for his particular purpose. This implied term can only be set aside where Angus can show that Jim was not relying on Angus's skill and judgment, or that it was unreasonable of Jim to rely on Angus's skill and judgment.

On the facts given in the question it would appear that Jim sought Angus's advice on vehicles to cope with tough conditions, and having done so it would appear that he was relying on Angus's skill and judgment (SOGA, s.14 (3)). As Angus knew Jim's farm, it would not be unreasonable to rely on Angus's skill and judgment. In this respect the situation is different from that in *Griffiths v Peter Conway Ltd* (1939), where the plaintiff failed to draw the seller's attention to the plaintiff's particular circumstances and accordingly the seller was not liable.

Angus might however claim that as Jim had had an opportunity to test the vehicle before he bought it, he was precluded from rejecting the vehicle later. It is true that Jim had such an opportunity, but he was not given the opportunity to drive it in the conditions that could exist at his farm, and it would not therefore be apparent that the vehicle might be unsuitable for those conditions (SOGA, s.14(2C)(b)). He could therefore claim damages (SOGA, s.15B(1)(a)) or treat the unsuitability of the car as a material breach and reject the goods (SOGA, s. 15B(1)(b)). It is arguable how material the breach is, but if he were a consumer, which by virtue of his being a farmer and acting in the course of his business he may not be (UCTA 1977, s.25(1)), he could not have the benefit of SOGA, s.15B(2) which would have given a clearer indication of the materiality qualification. It is arguable that Jim should have rejected the vehicle sooner. Under SOGA, s.34 Jim is allowed a reasonable opportunity to see if the vehicle is in accordance with his contract and, in particular, for the purpose for which he bought the vehicle. It is up to Jim to ask for the reasonable opportunity and the question does not say that he did ask for this. On the other hand, a month is not a very long time so it would have to be a matter of judgment for the court to decide whether or not a month was reasonable under the circumstances (SOGA, s.59) and in any case one of the effects of the Sale and Supply of Goods Regulations 2002 is to extend the period for the return of goods to six months (SOGA, s.48A), though this would only apply if Jim is deemed to be a consumer.

If Jim does succeed in claiming damages, he may claim for the loss directly and naturally arising out of the breach by Angus in providing a vehicle that failed to perform the purpose for which it was bought (SOGA, s.53A(1)).

Although in reality the dealer would no doubt repair the wipers free of charge, the failure of the wipers could be held to prevent the vehicle being of satisfactory quality, since under SOGA, s.14(2B), freedom from minor defects is one of the criteria used to establish satisfactory quality. This would in theory enable Jim to sue for damages under SOGA, s.15B(1), since non-working wipers could hardly be said to be a material breach of the contract. However, were Jim a consumer he would be able to reject the goods under section 15B(2) because of the wider definition of "material" in non-consumer contracts.

The inadvertent sale of the tow-truck is a sale by a seller in possession under SOGA, s.24. The second purchaser is entitled to keep the tow-truck and Jim is entitled to his money back.

2. *Consider the law applicable to the following situations:*

(a) *Ben steals a horse and sells it to Charles, who then sells it to David.*
(b) *Edith buys an antique chair from Frieda, paying for it with a cheque that subsequently is dishonoured by the bank. Edith then sells the chair to Gwen before Frieda tells Edith that the cheque is dishonoured and that she wants the chair back.*
(c) *Henry sends a consignment of barley to Ian for making whisky. Under the terms of their contract, Ian does not get the property in the barley until he has paid Henry. Ian then sells half the barley at a proper price to another whisky manufacturer who buys the barley unaware that Ian has not paid for it. The remaining half is still in Ian's possession when Ian is sequestrated.*
(d) *John, a wholesale meat merchant, undertakes to sell some specially selected frozen lamb to a restaurant which paid for it in advance. It was agreed that the risk would pass on payment. The lamb existed at the time the contract was made, but shortly after payment and before delivery to the restaurant, the electricity supply to the deepfreeze unit where the lamb was stored was cut off and the meat had to be destroyed.*
(e) *Keith shows Lottie, a consumer, a sample of his new industrial cleaners. They seem to be very effective, so Lottie orders a large supply. When they are duly delivered, Lottie signs the acceptance slip stating that she has accepted and examined the goods, even though in fact she did not have time to test them there and then. She also pays the haulier who delivered the goods. It transpires later that their cleaning ability is very poor.*

(a) In this situation, Ben has no right of ownership to pass to Charles. Charles does not obtain good title and can give no better title to David than he has. When the true owner finds his horse, he is entitled to claim it back from David as it never left his ownership. David can sue Charles for breach of the implied term in the SOGA 1979, s.12(1) that Charles had the right to sell the goods. A suitable case in point is *Rowland v Divell* (1923).

(b) Whereas question (a) dealt with a title that was void, (b) deals with a title that is voidable. Edith tricked Frieda into a fraudulent sale, but it remains a sale up to the point where Frieda challenges the sale. Under SOGA, s.23, where the title has not been avoided by the time of the sale to Gwen, Gwen acquires good title to the goods, provided she buys in good faith and without notice of the defect in Edith's title to the goods.

Accordingly Frieda's remedy, such as it is, is to find Edith and sue her for the value of the chair.

(c) The contract between Henry and Ian contains a retention of title clause, which in the normal course of events should ensure that while payment for the barley is still outstanding the barley remains in the ownership of Henry, even if it is in the possession of Ian. Accordingly the half of the barley that is remaining on Ian's sequestration must be returned to Henry as it never left Henry's ownership, and Ian's trustee in sequestration may not retain it. The barley that was sold to another whisky manufacturer will remain with the other manufacturer, provided he bought the barley in good faith and without any notice of any right of Henry's in the original barley (SOGA, s.25(1)). Henry would have to lodge a claim with Ian's trustee in sequestration for the value of the barley that had been sold on.

(d) This question refers to the perishing of goods. In this case there is no fault on either the buyer's or the seller's part, unless one takes the view that there ought to have been a back-up electricity generator. Assuming there is no fault, and given that the risk was specifically said to pass on payment, the restaurant has to bear the loss (SOGA, s.20(1)), and should have insured against the loss of the meat from the time of payment when the risk passed to the restaurant. If the power cut is attributable to the fault of John, he may be liable for the loss (SOGA, s.20(2)) and he may also be liable to the restaurant generally under a duty of care as a custodier of the meat (SOGA, s.20(3)). Note that this question is specifically not about consumers, since if the purchaser of the meat were a consumer, he would be protected under SOGA, s.20(4).

(e) This question concerns the buyer's right to examine the goods. Keith must allow Lottie a reasonable opportunity to examine the goods to see if they conform with the sample she was shown before (SOGA, s.34). Even though she apparently intimates that she has accepted the goods, under section 35 if she has not had the chance to examine them she is not deemed to have accepted the goods, and will not be deemed to have accepted the goods until she has carried out her examination (SOGA, s.35(2)), even if she agreed otherwise, as the contract in question is a consumer contract (SOGA, s.35(3)).

(As a general rule, in a question to do with sale and/or supply of goods, it is always wise to be alert to the wording of the question to see if the contract of sale is one which would be a consumer contract or not. Sometimes examiners will deliberately leave the point vague in order to see if students know both the law relating to businesses and to consumers.)

3. *(a)   Draw a diagram of a simple bill of exchange. Explain how a simple unindorsed bill of exchange operates. How can it be negotiated to another person?*

(b)   How does the law on bills of exchange serve to protect the holder in due course of a bill of exchange?

(c)   In what respects does a crossed cheque differ from a bill of exchange?

(d)   Suppose a bill of exchange was the required means of payment for some goods. If the goods were defective, could the drawee be instructed not to pay the bill?

(a) For an example bill of exchange, see page 31. A bill of exchange is an order in writing addressed by the drawer of the bill to the drawee (the person who is to pay the bill) requiring him to pay at a fixed or determinable date (which may be on demand, on sight, on a certain date, or on so many days after a certain date) a sum certain in money (which may include interest) to the payee or to the payee's order (Bills of Exchange Act 1882 ("BOE"), s.3). The payee may be the drawer.

Normally the drawer tells the drawee of the bill, and the drawee will accept the bill on a preliminary basis to acknowledge that he will have to pay the bill at the due date (at which stage the drawee becomes known as the acceptor). If the bill is a demand bill, acceptance does not arise and the bill should be paid on demand. Assuming that the bill is payable at a later date, the accepted bill is delivered to the payee. On the date for payment the bill will be presented for payment and payment will be made. This discharges the bill.

If the bill is not accepted, the payee may ultimately claim against the drawer for issuing him with a bill that the drawee cannot or will not accept (BOE, s.43(2)). If the bill is accepted but not paid, the payee may again claim against the drawer (BOE, s.47(2)).

Bills may be made payable to bearer, in which case they may be negotiated by delivery to someone else (BOE, s.31(2)), or they may be payable to the order of the payee. If they are marked non-negotiable, then anyone who takes the bill from the payee does so in the knowledge that he will get no better title to the bill than the payee (BOE, s.35). A bill made out to order means that the payee may, if he wishes, order someone else to have the benefit of the bill. He will do this by negotiating the bill to a transferee. This is done by indorsement which is signing the bill. The indorsee may in turn indorse the bill to someone else.

(b) A holder in due course is a person who has had a bill transferred to him. Provided he acquires the bill in good faith for a proper price, without notice of any defect in the transferor's title, and provided the bill is valid on the face of it and not overdue, he will be entitled to receive payment from the drawee, whom failing the drawer or any previous indorsee of the bill (BOE, s.29(1)). This places the holder in due course in a better position sometimes than the person who transferred the bill of exchange to him, and may mean that a person who has wrongfully obtained a bill of exchange may give a better title than he himself had. This rule does not apply where there has been forgery of any party's signature (BOE, s.24), though a drawee is not allowed to claim that a drawer's signature is forged by way of an attempt to avoid paying the bill (BOE, s.54(2)).

(c) A cheque differs little in principle from a bill of exchange, save that a cheque is always payable on demand and always drawn on a banker (BOE, s.73). Cheques are regulated by the BOE and by the Cheques Acts 1957 and 1992. Nowadays nearly all cheques are crossed which means that they may only be paid into a bank account. This means that a thief stealing a cheque would have to set up a bank account into which the cheque could be paid. Unlike bills of exchange, crossed cheques may not be indorsed. Cheques go stale after six months whereupon they need to be re-issued.

(d) A bill of exchange is a freestanding legal obligation in its own right irrespective of the underlying transaction for which it has been given. Furthermore, under BOE, s.3(1) it is an *unconditional* order in writing, so it is not permissible to include any clause that makes payment dependent on the quality of the goods.

4. *Charles wishes to insure his domestic property and approaches his insurance broker to help him obtain the best quotations. He also wants to take out some life assurance and wants any proceeds of the life assurance policy to be paid to his wife if he dies within the term of the policy. Charles notices that in the domestic insurance proposal form he is required to warrant that his house is wind and watertight at the time of the commencement of the policy, and that he will take all steps to keep it so. He also notices that it is a material condition of the life assurance proposal that he is in good health. He tells his agent that he is suffering from high blood pressure and that his doctor has warned him that he must take life easy. The agent ignores this fact and writes down that Charles is in good health. Charles sees this but signs it anyway. Two weeks after the policy has commenced, Charles drops dead of a heart attack.*
Explain what the law is in relation to the above matters.

A broker is a person who acts as a middleman between the insurance company and the insured. He is normally paid by commission from the insurance company. The law is unclear as to whether the broker can be treated in law as the insurer's agent or the insured's agent, but where there is a tied agency the supposition is that the broker will be the insurer's agent.

It is perfectly possible for the life assurance policy to be written in trust for Charles's wife (Married Women's Policies of Assurance (Scotland) Act 1880).

A warranty is a statement which need not be material but which must be strictly complied with, as in *Dawson v Bonnin*. However, to undertake to take all steps to keep the house wind and watertight is not easy and one would normally expect the proposer to be able to qualify that warranty by undertaking to take all "reasonable" steps to keep the building wind and watertight.

As regards Charles's health, even though the broker completed the proposal inaccurately Charles should have corrected it since he is under a requirement to act in the utmost good faith (*uberrimae fidei*) in the completion of the form, as in *The Spathari*. Accordingly his false declaration invalidates the policy.

5. (a) Eve, a director of a wine bottling company, is buying a country cottage in the Highlands. She cannot afford to pay for it all herself so she takes out a loan from the bank. The bank requires her to grant a standard security over the cottage in favour of the bank. Explain to Eve what this means and what the bank's rights are in respect of this standard security.

(b) Eve's company owns a large quantity of wine in large sealed vats. The wine is stored in warehouses in Leith until the time comes to bottle the wine. The wine in the vats is valuable and as the company is needing funds for expansion of its operations, Eve and her fellow directors wonder if it is possible for the company to raise a loan on the strength of the value of wine at present in the warehouses. The bank agrees to lend on the strength of the value of the wine in the vats, but is unsure how to take security over the wine. How could this be done?

(a) A standard security is a charge over land. It must be registered in the Register of Sasines or the Land Register as the case may be. It is granted by Eve in favour of the bank and serves to prevent Eve selling the cottage without first obtaining the discharge of the standard security, unless the purchaser is unwise enough to buy the cottage subject to Eve's standard security, which would be unlikely. The standard security will normally only be discharged once the bank has been repaid its loan, interest and any expenses. If Eve fails to maintain what would in England be called her mortgage payments, the bank could take the steps open to it in terms of the standard security documentation to repossess the cottage, evict Eve and her belongings and sell the cottage. Alternatively, the bank could foreclose on the property, which is to sell the property with the intention of keeping it for itself, thus preventing Eve from redeeming the property.

(b) In this situation, the bank could either receive a pledge of the wine in the vats in the warehouse, or it could be given a floating charge over the company's assets, including the wine. If there is a pledge, the vats must be clearly identifiable, separated from other persons' vats, and physically unavailable to Eve's company (perhaps by being fenced off and locked, with the key being given to the bank) except with the express permission of the bank as its agent for such necessary purposes as, say, maintenance. It must not be open to Eve's company to abstract wine from time to time and to bottle and sell it (see *West Lothian Oil Co. (in liquidation) v Mair*). This procedure would give the bank a fixed charge over the wine which would be valid against a liquidator or any other creditor. In terms of Companies Act 1985 s.410 the pledge of the wine is an unregistrable charge and would only be registered in the company's own register of charges, not in the public register available at the office of the Registrar of Companies.

A more common remedy would be for the company to grant the bank a floating charge over the company's assets, including the wine in the vats. By this means the company would have much greater freedom to continue dealing in the wine. Providing the company's net assets were always greater than the value of the loan, the bank would be unlikely to have any difficulty with this. Under the legislation at the time of writing, if the company defaulted on the repayment of the loan, the bank would appoint a receiver under the Insolvency Act 1986, s.52, who would proceed to sell the wine, and any other asset of the company caught by the crystallised floating charge, to recoup the loss to the bank, subject to payment of any prior-ranking claims, including preferential debts, under the Insolvency Act 1986, s.60.

A floating charge would need to be registered at the office of the Registrar of Companies within 21 days of its creation (Companies Act 1985, s.410). Without registration the floating charge would be void against another creditor, liquidator or administrator.

Under the legislation anticipated under the Enterprise Act 2002, and assuming the bank's floating charge was granted after the implementation of that Act, the Bank's remedy on default would be to appoint an administrator on two days' notice, irrespective of the solvency of the company. The role of the administrator would be the survival of the company as a going concern, which failing the administrator should aim to help all creditors including, ultimately, the bank.

6. *Jim, a tradesman, is unfortunately in financial difficulties. He has total assets of £60,000, of which the major part is his own home which he shares with his wife. The house is entirely in his own name and is worth £40,000. He owns no other heritage, though he leases a lock-up garage from Keepo Ltd He pays Keepo Ltd rent of £300 a month. In the garage he keeps the tools of this trade and some antique furniture that he is hoping to restore. Sadly he has had little business recently and has not been paying his bills.*

By June 1, 20X3 the following matters have arisen:

(a)   he is three months behind on the rent for the garage;

(b) he transferred his home to his wife by means of a disposition recorded in the Land Register on May 1, 20X3;

(c) on May 20, 20X3 he repaid his brother Tony a loan of £5,000 which, according to the terms of their loan agreement, was not due to be repaid until March 1, 20X4;

(d) he was due to pay Tools-R-Us Ltd £3,000 for various items, the payment date being April 1, 20X3;

(e) he failed to account to H.M. Customs and Excise for the sum of £4,000 in respect of outstanding VAT also due on April 1, 20X3;

(f) Big Supplies plc, which had not received payment of the sum of £5,000, arrested his bank account with the Bank of Inchcolm and obtained funds from it on May 15, 20X3;

(g) Cut-purse, a loan shark, has insisted that the £5,000 loan Jim borrowed from him at a rate of 20 per cent per annum should now have its interest rate increased to 40 per cent to take account of Jim's uncertain financial prospects.

Jim's accountant successfully petitions the court for an award of sequestration, dated June 1, 20X3, against Jim on the grounds that he failed to pay outstanding accounting fees of £5,000.

Under these circumstances, what points of law apply to the above?

This question refers to bankruptcy which is governed by the Bankruptcy (Scotland) Act 1985 ("BSA"). Jim is sequestrated with effect from June 1, 20X3 and an interim trustee will be appointed to safeguard his assets; in due course a permanent trustee will be vested in those assets. Given the size of the assets it is possible that he could repay in full all his creditors, but from the information given it would appear that he is both practically insolvent and by virtue of the award of sequestration apparently insolvent.

(a) If Keepo Ltd proceeds to a sequestration for rent, the landlord's hypothec will defeat the trustee in sequestration (BSA, s.33(2)). Accordingly the landlord would ultimately be able to seize and sell the antique furniture in the garage, though not the tools of Jim's trade.

(b) As the disposition in favour of his wife took place one month before the date of sequestration, it falls within the five-year period required for a gratuitous alienation to an associate (BSA, s.34). The trustee could apply to court to reduce the disposition and have the house returned to the debtor's estate. The trustee could not necessarily immediately force Jim and his wife out of the house since they need somewhere to live, but ultimately, if necessary, the trustee may be able to force the sale of the house (BSA, s.40), subject to the court's protection of Jim's family.

(c) This repayment would be an unfair preference under BSA, s.36 and Tom would be required to return the loan. Tom would merely become an ordinary creditor.

(d) Tools-R-Us are merely ordinary creditors. They obtain no privileged position relative to other creditors.

(e) By contrast, H.M. Customs and Excise are preferred creditors and will be repaid out of the debtor's estate in priority to the ordinary creditors (BSA, s.51(1)(e)).

(f) Sequestration acts as if a completed diligence for all creditors had taken place simultaneously on the date of sequestration. Big Supplies plc are effectively ordinary creditors, but they will be able to obtain their expenses (BSA, s.37(5)). The diligence they effected will be equalised with all the other creditors.

(g) This is an extortionate credit transaction and the court could insist that the terms of the loan be rewritten and that the creditor only be entitled to a reasonable rate of interest (BSA, s.61). The capital that was lent is yet another debt due by Jim and the trustee will place it with the other debts.

The accountant who sequestrates Jim will be allowed the expenses of his petition against Jim as a prior claim against Jim's estate, but the £5,000 he is due will be yet another unsecured debt.

The trustee in sequestration will ingather as much of Jim's estate as he can, will pay the preferential creditors and prior creditors and then, depending on whether or not the estate is solvent, will pay the creditors in full if possible or in proportion to their claims if not.

7. Consider the points of law arising out of the following situation:

Martin's electronics business has just completed 10 successful years, and he wishes to have a large and splendid garden party to celebrate. While he is confident in the realm of computers, he is less so in the realm of corporate hospitality, and so asks Senga to organise the party for him, as he does not have time to arrange all the details himself. He explains that he wants marquees, plenty of good quality wine, canapes, children's entertainments, jazz bands, etc.

As Martin has a high opinion of Senga he asks her personally to arrange all this for him. He gives her a budget and expects her to keep within it. There is no mention of a fee for her services in the budget, and when she asks about her fee, he says he will get back to her about that but fails to do so.

Senga's little brother, Sam, has newly set up a lighting business and she asks him to deal with the lighting and sound system. She asks him for a commission of only 5 per cent (she would normally have asked 10 per cent) for obtaining the work for him. Her other brother, Bill, runs a marquee erection and hire service through a limited company, in which she has a 25 per cent shareholding. She asks his company to put up the marquees. Although Martin did not ask her to do so, she arranged for floodlighting of the grounds and for a water feature to serve as a backdrop to the evening.

Come the evening, the party goes very well until the unfortunate moment when Martin accidentally drops a glass of water on some wiring and fatally electrocutes himself. As none of his family is with him, everyone looks to Senga to sort things out. As the band will not leave until they have been paid, she pays them out of her own pocket since they inevitably want cash.

After the funeral the bills for the party come in. Martin's executors have misgivings about some of the items and announce that until Senga produces proper accounts no funds will be disbursed to her or anyone else.

This question is about agency. There are no special requirements for creating a contract of agency, and although there is no sum set down for her remuneration Senga would normally be entitled to be paid on a *quantum meruit* basis in the absence of any agreement to the contrary.

However, she has not necessarily exercised her fiduciary duty to Martin in the way that she should. She obtained a secret profit from her brother (as in *Boston Deep Sea Fishing Ltd v Ansell* (1888)) which should properly have been disclosed to Martin. Likewise her interest in the marquee company run by Bill should have been disclosed to Martin for his approval, since there is a conflict of interest there as well (see *McPherson's Trs v Watt* (1877)). Her use of the floodlighting and water feature raises the issue of whether she had the apparent authority to hire such items on Martin's behalf. The question does not state whether he approved of these items, but if he did (which is likely, since he must have noticed them during the party), he would be deemed to have ratified her actions, in which case Martin's estate would be liable for their cost. Even if he did not approve, and if the floodlight and water feature installers had no reason to think that these items were not within Senga's authority to order, his estate would still be liable since her lack of authority had not been communicated to them (see *Watteau v Fenwick* (1892)). When Senga paid the band's fees following Martin's sudden death it is arguable that she was acting as an agent of necessity as something had to be done in a hurry and there was no one with the requisite authority to act on his or his estate's behalf.

Finally it is certainly the case that Senga would need to produce accounts for all her intromissions and expenditure, this being part of her general duty to Martin and the estate.

8. *Three sisters, Effie, Ishbel and Morag wish to set up a laundry business. The idea is that they will visit clients' houses, uplift their clients' laundry and deliver it to them the same day cleaned, ironed, and sorted out. They open a partnership account and each put in £200. They buy a new washing machine, tumble drier, iron and ironing board. All the work is done in Effie's house, as she has the biggest laundry room; the collection and delivery is done in Ishbel's car; while Morag, who is the*

most personable, is the one who deals with the clients on the telephone and in person. They call their firm "The Three Graces".

Although after six months the firm is showing a certain profit, it is not enough for Effie's liking. She takes it upon herself to branch out into other forms of cleaning, such as dry-cleaning furniture and repairing clothes. She does not tell her sisters about this, even though most of her customers came through the business. She keeps the income from this work to herself. One day she does some furniture cleaning work for herself but makes a poor job of it. The owner of the badly cleaned furniture then proposes to sue the firm, not least because the owner has a receipt from Donald, Effie's bankrupt husband (and who sometimes helps her), signing "The Three Graces" apparently on behalf of the firm, confirming payment from the furniture owner to Effie. Having been unaware of Effie's new line of business, Ishbel and Morag are furious when they hear of this. They say that Donald had no business signing receipts on behalf of the firm and that he alone is liable.

Ishbel believes that as she is doing all the driving and she is paying for the petrol she should be entitled to a greater share of the profits than the one-third share which they have verbally agreed they each should take out from the business. She also believes that neither the wear and tear on the car nor her insurance is being properly recompensed, so she takes money out of the firm bank account whenever she is a bit short. She is not very good about keeping records of her withdrawals from the bank account. When challenged she claims that she is repaying herself her expenses, not receiving her drawings.

Morag decides that in her free time she should set up an escort agency, and believing that a bank would be unlikely to fund her she approaches a small local finance shop for funds. She explains what she needs the money for and the finance shop says that it will lend her the money provided the finance shop can have a deposit from the firm of the Three Graces and that the firm will pay an interest rate of 21 per cent. Morag explains that she cannot produce a deposit, but she on behalf of the firm will give the finance shop a promissory note undertaking to repay the capital sum and interest at the desired rate. Morag fails to tell her sisters about the promissory note, but shortly before the due date for repayment of the promissory note Effie disappears with all the firm's funds anyway.

What is the legal position relating to all this?

When Effie embarks on another business she will probably try to say that it is unconnected with the business of the Three Graces. On the other hand, under the Partnership Act 1890, s.29, she should disclose any private profits accruing to her through the use of the firm's business connections and name. Effie would be required to hand over any secret profits to the firm. It is arguable that the failure to prevent Donald representing himself as authorised to sign documents, even though it was not with the approval of Ishbel and Morag, could, as far as outsiders are concerned, be construed as holding Donald out to be authorised. As far as

the annoyed furniture owner is concerned he had no reason to doubt that
Donald was authorised, and would be able to assert his rights under the
Partnership Act, s.14 since he believed that Donald was either a partner,
or, under general rules of agency, that Donald had apparent authority to
do as he was doing. As Donald is not worth suing, it makes sense for the
furniture owner to sue the firm since it could probably satisfy her decree.
If the firm's assets were insufficient, each partner would be jointly and
severally liable to the client for the debt arising from the client's claim
(Partnership Act 1890, s.9).

As regards Ishbel, she has forgotten that there is a duty on each partner
under the Partnership Act 1890, s.28 to render true accounts and disclose
to her fellow partners all matters affecting the firm. She should be
keeping proper records, and although she is indeed entitled to her
expenses under section 24(2) (in the absence of any rules to the contrary),
this does not give her permission to treat the accounts lightly.

Morag's loan cannot be described as being in the ordinary course of
business, and accordingly under the Partnership Act, s. 5 there is no
reason for the partnership to be liable as it must have been apparent, on
the principle of *Paterson Bros v Gladstone* (1891) that Morag was not
authorised to pledge the firm's credit in this way. So the firm would not
be liable anyway, which is probably just as well since Effie has taken all
its money. The two other sisters could sue Effie for the money if they can
find her.

9. *Emmeline, Fingal and Genista run a partnership together making
tartan souvenirs for tourists. On their accountants' advice they decide to
incorporate the business as a limited liability company. They had been
equal partners, but for various domestic reasons, Emmeline decides that
she wants to subscribe for only a few shares in the company, though she
is willing to lend money to the company.*

*The company has an authorised share capital of £1,000. Emmeline
takes 100 ordinary £1.00 nominal value shares and Fingal and Genista
each take 450 ordinary £1.00 nominal value shares. In addition
Emmeline agrees to lend £3,500 to the company in the form of a loan
repayable in five years' time with a coupon of 8 per cent. All three
shareholders are appointed directors.*

*The company starts to trade with Table A as its articles of association.
Negotiations continue between the shareholders. It is thought appropriate
that Emmeline should obtain some security for her loan. It is also agreed
that all decisions taken by the directors should be unanimous and that no
other shareholders should be admitted without the consent of all
shareholders. However, no documentation is ever finalised or signed to
reflect these agreements as none of the three has time to look at these
matters in detail.*

*Almost immediately after incorporation problems arise. Emmeline
wishes to withdraw her money from the company. The shareholders fall
out with each other and lose all confidence in each other.*

What should have been done, but was not, and what could be done now? Advise the three directors.

What should have been done

In an ideal world, the company should have drawn up its own version of its articles, based on Table A, but altered to reflect the desires of the three shareholders. Given that Emmeline has fewer shares than the others, it would have been sensible for her to have a class of shares whose rights could not have been altered by the other two shareholders (Companies Act 1985, s.125). One of the rights attaching to her shares would have been that the other shareholders may not improve their own rights (since the other shareholders effectively are a class of shares in their own right too) relative to hers. Any alteration of their rights would require her approval. The second thing to build in would be weighted voting (on the principle of *Bushell v Faith* (1970)), so that no two shareholders could "gang up" on the third. This would effectively also force the shareholders to work in concert. An alternative method would be to have three classes of shares with a deadlock agreement forcing them to vote unanimously or not at all, failing which the issue could be referred to arbitration or the company could be wound up. A second alternative would have been to draw up a shareholders' agreement reflecting the shareholders' agreed practice.

If Emmeline wishes to have security for her loan, she may do this, and she could have a standard security over heritage, if the company has any, or a floating charge over its assets. The problem with a floating charge is that if it is granted within two years of the company's insolvent liquidation, the floating charge may be reducible at the instance of the liquidator because Emmeline is a "connected person"; hence the loan must be genuinely made for value to the company (Insolvency Act 1986, s.245). Notwithstanding this caveat, there is no reason why she should not have the benefit of a charge, but if it is to be a standard security in her favour, it must be registered within 21 days of the registration of the standard security in the Register of Sasines or Land Register (as the case may be) or, if a floating charge, 21 days from the date of execution of the floating charge (Companies Act 1985, s.410). Assuming the charge is validly registered, then in the event of the company's insolvency she could sell the heritable property or appoint a receiver (Insolvency Act 1986, s.51). For the position post-Enterprise Act 2002, see the final paragraph of the answer to question 5, above.

The current position

Under the existing circumstances, the best thing to do would be for the members to co-operate sufficiently to have the company wound up following a voluntary resolution by the members to that effect under the Insolvency Act 1986, s.84(1)(b). If the company is solvent, all the creditors will be repaid and everyone should get their money back. If the members have lost all confidence in each other and the basis of their agreement is gone, it is possible to have the company wound up on just and equitable grounds (Insolvency Act 1986, s.122(1)(g) (as in *Ebrahimi v Westbourne Galleries* Ltd (1973)). It is also open to Emmeline to petition the court for a winding-up order for repayment of her loan (Insolvency Act 1986, s.122(1)(f)), but in each case it would clearly be an expensive way for the company of getting her money back, not least because there would be court fees on top of a liquidator's fees to deal with.

10. *Tom is an inventor. He designs a new type of clockwork CD player. He wants to protect all the intellectual property in his new invention and to prevent other people copying his invention. What should he do?*

Tom needs to patent his invention with the Patent Office. This may take some time and while it is in the process of being patented there is always the danger of other people coming up with a similar idea, which while not necessarily impairing the patentability of his invention, may make it less marketable. In order to be patented, his invention must be new, involve an inventive step and be capable of industrial application (Patents Act 1977, s.1). He would probably need to use a patent agent to help him apply for a patent. Once his invention was patented, he could take action by way of interdict or a claim for damages against anyone who copied or misused his invention (Patents Act ss.60-71). The patent is protected for twenty years (Patents Act s.25).

He could also obtain copyright in his instruction manuals which describe how to operate and repair the clockwork CD. There is no register of copyright, but under the Copyright, Designs and Patents Act 1988 he would need to assert his right of copyright by taking action against anyone who copied his wording. The wording would need to be original. The copyright endures for seventy years after Tom's death (s.12).

If his new invention has a trade mark, he would be well advised to have the trade mark registered in the Register of Trade Marks (Copyright Design and Patents Act 1988). This protects the trade mark for ten years.

If there is a particular new feature of the design on the CD player, such as its distinctive casing or decoration, not particularly pertinent to the operation of the CD player itself, it would be possible to protect that too for up to fifteen years by means of registration under the Registered Designs Act 1949 or by means of the unregistered right under the Copyright Design and Patents Act 1988. Although it is possible to protect the overall design, it is not possible to prevent others from making spare parts.

INDEX

111